863   Lindstrom, Naomi,
LIN   1950-

Jorge Luis Borges

$19.95

DATE			

JORGE
LUIS
BORGES
A Study of the Short Fiction

Naomi Lindstrom
University of Texas at Austin

TWAYNE PUBLISHERS • BOSTON
A Division of G. K. Hall & Co.

Twayne's Studies in Short Fiction Series No. 16

Copyright 1990 by G. K. Hall & Co.
All rights reserved.
Published by Twayne Publishers
A division of G. K. Hall & Co.
70 Lincoln Street
Boston, Massachusetts 02111

Copyediting supervised by Barbara Sutton.
Book design and production by Janet Z. Reynolds.
Typeset in 10 pt. Caslon 540
by Crane Typesetting Service, West Barnstable, Massachusetts

First published 1990.
10 9 8 7 6 5 4 3 2 1

The paper used in this publication meets the minimum requirements
of American National Standard for Information Sciences—Permanence
of Paper for Printed Library Materials, ANSI Z39.48-1984. ∞™

Printed and bound in the United States of America.

Library of Congress Cataloging-in-Publication Data

Lindstrom, Naomi, 1950–
    Jorge Luis Borges : a study of the short fiction / Naomi
Lindstrom.
        p.   cm.—(Twayne's studies in short fiction ; no. 16)
    Includes bibliographical references.
    ISBN 0-8057-8327-X (alk. paper)
    1. Borges, Jorge Luis, 1899-   —Criticism and interpretation.
I. Title.   II. Series.
PQ7797.B635Z7735   1990
863—dc20   90-4155
                                                                CIP

To Frederick B. Lindstrom

Contents

Preface

As writer, reader, judge, and commentator on literature, Jorge Luis Borges maintained a complex, at times conflict-ridden and paradoxical, relationship with short fiction—the form in which he achieved his international fame. Since childhood, he was a rapt but also critically alert reader of the short story and of such parallel narrative types as the fable, the parable, the legend, and the spoken supernatural anecdote. He developed strong, though often revised, beliefs about the ways in which short fiction could best fulfill its potential and, as an arbiter of tastes, sought to instill these tenets in the minds of the Argentine reading public.

Nonetheless, during the first decade of his literary career (the 1920s), Borges was known as a poet. Even after he had largely abandoned the writing of poetry, disillusioned with the avant-garde aesthetic that had guided his verse efforts, Borges did not immediately turn to the short story, a seemingly natural step given his long-standing personal ties to the genre. Instead, he devised a number of variant types of the essay, incorporating more and more features of imaginative writing. These experiments, which began to occupy Borges during the first half of the 1930s, brought him by approximations to the writing, in the mid-1930s, of what was essentially brief fiction. Still, such was his hesitancy about attempting work in this genre that, in his own mind, it was not until 1939 that he began his career as a short story writer.

Even once he was undeniably working in short fiction, Borges continued to vary the form by commingling its characteristics with those of expository prose. A number of his most distinctive stories present themselves as reports, articles in reference works, or journal entries. For all their look of documentary factualism, these texts reveal themselves to have been "authored" under fictitious circumstances by imaginary writers. Even when he does not pretend that his stories are documents he is reproducing, Borges transfers many features of expository writing to short fiction. The story may include ostensibly erudite annotations or scientific findings, or narration may give way to what at first appear to be Borges's own observations. Far from removing the short story from the realm of artfully created work, this hybridization makes the texts' nature as artistic invention, and even illusion, stand out more vividly.

This vein of innovation is particularly prominent in the stories of Borges's two celebrated collections, *Ficciones* (1944, expanded 1956; translated as *Ficciones*, 1962) and *El Aleph* (1949, expanded 1952; translated as *The Aleph*, 1970). These two volumes, containing between them the stories Borges wrote at the height of his creative powers, are recognized as among the most distinctive and original contributions made to the evolution of the genre in the twentieth century.

Ficciones and *The Aleph* continue to form the basis of Borges's still-growing fame, and many readers still associate Borges exclusively with the type of short fiction collected in the two volumes. Reading only these stories, it would be easy to conclude that a "typical" Borges story unfailingly displays the qualities of irony, paradox, and ambiguity that abound in the stories of the high period, relying, as always, on their generally baroque style and textual construction and giving out information cryptically through allusions to such emblematic items as labyrinths, mirrors, swords, towers, circular objects, and red chambers. Having worked out this set of narrative resources, though, Borges later abandoned the greater part of it. After adding a few similar stories to expanded editions of *Ficciones* and *The Aleph*, Borges by 1954 had ceased to publish new fiction, with the exception of work done in collaboration and in a lighter vein. When he resumed publishing stories of his own, beginning in 1966, it soon became apparent that his approach to narrative had undergone a profound alteration.

The fiction contained in Borges's two late collections, *El informe de Brodie* (1970; *Doctor Brodie's Report*, 1972) and *El libro de arena* (1975; *The Book of Sand*, 1977), proved a shock to many longtime readers of his short fiction. Borges had moved away from the baroque aesthetic evident in the often-convoluted and intricately constructed stories. He now drew less upon the repertory of devices typical of self-conscious, high-art authors. Instead, he paid an imitative homage to humbler taletellers while remaining a distinctly literary artist. Borges had designed many of his new texts to resemble unpretentious narratives principally concerned with plot: ghost stories told by the hearth, personal reminiscences of encounters with the uncanny, or lore handed down from the great pagan cultures of northern Europe. His earlier stories had been impossible for readers or critics to summarize without attempting to resolve ambiguities and, in effect, carrying out an interpretation. In the case of the new stories, it was possible to extract from each an uncluttered narrative line—quite often, one that could serve well in an exchange of tales around the camp fire.

In treating the tales produced in the latter stretch of Borges's career, the goal has been to do justice to them both as autonomous creations and as evidence of the new direction taken by the author of the famous earlier stories. The discussion is meant to bring out the special strengths of the late stories. Especially significant are their appealing, though clearly disingenuous, mimicry of plain speech and homespun tale-telling, their ability to convey a sense of ancient magic, and the possibilities they offer for symbolic interpretation. Nonetheless, it is difficult to avoid the conclusion that Borges's second series of stories offers, on the whole, less material for analysis than the first does. It would be unfair to both sets of short fiction to try to claim for the late works a density and complexity equal to that of their better-known predecessors.

Whereas this study focuses greatest attention on the oblique, involved texts of *Ficciones* and *The Aleph*, which gained for Borges a place in the history of short fiction, an effort has been made to portray Borges's evolving thought about and practice of short fiction throughout his lifetime. In this context—after Borges's high period of the late 1930s to early 1950s—the late 1960s and early 1970s are the most important years in his development as a short story writer, followed by the early period of Borges's relation to short fiction, from about 1930, after he had virtually abandoned poetry, to the late 1930s, when he finally took the definitive step of becoming a short story writer (though he had published work in this genre as early as 1933). During this time, Borges devised a number of mutations of the short essay. In his book reviews and cultural journalism, he went beyond the degree of imaginative elaboration customarily allowed in these types of writings. The most extended result of this line of experimentation are the stories of criminal careers that make up the bulk of *Historia universal de la infamia* (1935; *A Universal History of Infamy*, 1970). Accounts from diverse sources are presented as factual but have received a thoroughly creative reworking in the telling. This aspect of Borges's writing is here treated, above all, as an indication of the process that led to the development of the renowned stories of *Ficciones* and *The Aleph*.

Much briefer attention goes to Borges's other, more peripheral ventures into short fiction. These include his stories written in collaboration —most significantly, those co-written with Adolfo Bioy Casares. Another sideline was the retelling of brief narratives culled from diverse sources, such as legends, parables, and accounts of dreams, fantasies, and extraordinary experiences, whether his own or others'. Also deserving of mention are the influential short story anthologies Borges edited together with Bioy and, on occasion, Silvina Ocampo; these helped spread an ideal of distanced, nonmimetic, and rigorously constructed short fiction. In his eagerness to shape the fiction-reading public's tastes, as well as to work out his own continually evolving aesthetic, Borges championed different authors' work. His enthusiasm for Kafka's short stories, which he sought to bring to a Spanish-language readership, is among the most noteworthy examples of Borges's often-profound engagement with the short fiction of his predecessors. Thus, care has been taken to treat Borges not solely as one who worked in brief fiction—as writer, commentator, anthologist, and translator—but also as a lifelong member of the appreciative reading public.

Naomi Lindstrom

University of Texas at Austin

Acknowledgments

Carter Wheelock's "Borges and the 'Death' of the Text" first appeared in *Hispanic Review* 53 (1985): 151–61. Reprinted by permission.

David William Foster's "Borges and Structuralism: Toward an Implied Poetics" first appeared in *Modern Fiction Studies* 19, no. 3 (1973): 341–51. © 1973 by Purdue Research Foundation, West Lafayette, Indiana. Reprinted by permission.

Fernando Sorrentino's interview with Borges first appeared in English in *Seven Conversations with Jorge Luis Borges*, trans. Clark M. Zlotchew (Troy, N.Y.: Whitston Publishing Co., 1982); the original Spanish-language edition, *Siete conversaciones con Jorge Luis Borges*, was published by Casa Pardo of Buenos Aires in 1973. Reprinted by permission of Fernando Sorrentino and Clark M. Zlotchew.

Support for the research and writing of this work came from the Dallas TACA Centennial Fellowship in Liberal Arts, University of Texas at Austin.

I would like to acknowledge the influence of two Borges scholars with whom I have had professional and friendly associations of many years' standing, as well as being a reader of their criticism. Anyone familiar with the work and thought of Carter Wheelock and David William Foster will no doubt recognize the many ways in which their readings of Borges have colored mine.

Part 1

THE SHORT FICTION

Edging toward the Short Story

Although Jorge Luis Borges won his international fame as an innovator in the short story, deliberately rejecting the novel as a vehicle for his narrative prose, a look at his career shows that he was slow to come to the genre. Indeed, for many years he seemed anxious to avoid the role of short story writer, despite his expressed fascination with the form, and only approached it in an oblique fashion. Like most members of his literary generation in Argentina—and like nearly all of his colleagues in the Buenos Aires avant-garde—Borges made his name in the 1920s with verse as his medium for imaginative expression. From the early 1920s, when he first gained recognition, well into the 1930s, Borges reserved prose exclusively for expository writing. His first three book-length creative works are collections of self-consciously innovative po-etry, dated 1923, 1925, and 1929. Toward the end of the twenties, he lost all confidence in experimental verse and authored very little poetry for many years thereafter. Martin S. Stabb notes that, in 1929, Borges ceased for several months to appear in print and then reemerged as almost strictly a writer of essays and criticism. He published no poetry until 1934, then began to release a few poetic texts at considerable intervals.[1] Having nearly dropped poetry and as yet unready to begin authoring short stories, Borges was left nearly without a genre of cre-ative literature in which to work, or at least one in which he was willing to publish his efforts. This situation, no doubt a difficult one for a literary creator, prevailed during the years leading up to Borges's un-interrupted run of highly original work in the short story (from the late 1930s to the early 1950s).

In expository writing, the youthful Borges produced four sets of brief commentaries on literary and philosophical matters (1925, 1926, 1928, and 1932) and a literary biography, the 1930 *Evaristo Carriego*, which is essentially an impressionistic evocation of Buenos Aires street cul-ture. Borges later regarded his early work with some shame; he omitted portions of it from his complete works and discouraged translations. The exceptions are the two very latest works. The 1930 biography appeared in English in 1983 as *Evaristo Carriego: A Book about Old-*

Time Buenos Aires. The 1932 *Discusión* continued to interest its author; he revised rather than abandoned it, and permitted translations into French and Italian.

Though he appeared strictly a poet and essayist during his first decade on the Buenos Aires literary scene, Borges had long been developing a repertory that would distinctly mark his stories. He had early gained considerable experience in the reading and evaluation of short fiction and in the composition of narrative prose. His father, who had a long history of frustration as a writer, was eager for his son to develop into a literary man.[2] The elder Borges made available his fine private library. Here Borges learned to read from English-language texts. Later he liked to recall his bookish childhood as a time of astounding tales and adventure stories, as well as more substantial fiction. He became a reader of Edgar Allan Poe, Robert Louis Stevenson, Mark Twain, and H. G. Wells—authors who would continue to serve him as points of reference. Some of the lesser known short story writers he later championed in his literary criticism were originally childhood enthusiasms, as in the case of Bret Harte and his tales of frontier California. *Don Quixote* made a particular impression. Borges, first excited by the vivid action of its episodes, matured into an astute reader of Cervantes and included insightful allusions to *Don Quixote* in both his essays and his fiction. He recalls that, when he first turned to writing, he thought of exciting readers with an inventive story. The earliest text Borges remembers authoring is a story, resembling the adventures narrated in Don Quixote and bearing the title "La visera fatal" (The fatal helmet). In giving his earliest publication, Borges enjoyed citing his translation, carried out as a small child, of Oscar Wilde's fable "The Happy Prince." These reminiscences suggest that Borges first thought of literature primarily as fiction.

During Borges's adolescence, when his family spent the war years in Switzerland, he was struck by the avant-garde poetry movements sweeping Europe and became an enthusiast of experimental verse. His remembered readings during this period also include philosophical treatises, autobiographies and personal essays, novels, and short stories. One of Borges's unusual tastes in short fiction, the detective tales of G. K. Chesterton, dates to this period. But poetry came to assume prime importance in his reading. As he began to gain proficiency in reading German, he came upon the expressionist poetry that was then the most spectacular new development in German-language literature. This highly metaphorical, emotive, disjointed verse, which reflected an obsession with linguistic and expressive originality, so impressed Borges that he determined to attempt a similar innovation in Spanish. A subsequent stay in Spain, in 1919–21, brought Borges into contact with the Ultraístas. The young poets who constituted this extreme avant-garde group produced little work of lasting value but were important in bringing an experimental spirit to Spanish-language poetry. Like the expressionists, the Spanish avant-gardists prized the invention of unusual metaphors and devalued the continuity to which narrative prose tends. Consequently, they favored poetry and aphorism over fiction. Borges began publishing poetry while peripherally associated with this movement, but subsequently urged students of his work to disregard these efforts as juvenilia previous to the start of his career.

In reviewing the sources of Borges's literary thought and of the unusual reservoir of knowledge referred to in his stories, commentators have often cited a pattern of personal contacts and readings that began during his years in Switzerland and Spain. Jewish culture and issues claimed Borges's attention through friendships with Jewish schoolmates in Geneva. The idea of a cultural tradition placing such a high value on the reading and discussion of texts and, generally, on learning exercised great appeal. The first novel Borges managed to read in German was *Der Golem* (*The Golem*) by Gustav Meyrinck. Set in Prague, this expressionistic work of 1915 adapts, for literary purposes, the legend of the Golem, a man created from nonliving matter through cabalistic means. Cabala would become a recurring topic in Borges's short stories. One of the most famous, "Las ruinas circulares" ("The Circular Ruins"), is a reworking of the Golem theme, while others involve such cabalistic concepts as the alphabet as an instrument of creation and source of esoteric forces. Edna Aizenberg has done a valuable job of tracing this connection in her 1984 *The Aleph Weaver: Biblical, Kabbalistic and Judaic Elements in Borges*, particularly her chapter "A Vindication of the Kabbalah."[3]

In Spain, among many literary associations Borges later deemed worthless, he formed one bond that he would continue to see as important to his development. This was his relation with the person and work of Rafael Cansino-Asséns, a poet and essayist who became something of a tribal elder to the young Ultraístas. This eccentric man of letters had become obsessed with Spain's Jewish past. Although Cansino-Asséns's ancestral link with the Sephardic world was uncertain, his devotion to this connection was thorough—an anomaly in an era when even Spain's intellectuals were often apt to deny any personal traces of Jewish identity or collective influence from the Jewish civilization that had flowered in their country. Aizenberg (18–22) argues for recognizing the importance of Borges's association with this odd figure, whose preoccupation with Judaica produced such notably uneven results.

On his 1921 return to Argentina, Borges began organizing a movement in Buenos Aires to parallel the European avant-gardes. The participants were, in most cases, poets and painters. Borges's interest in authoring fiction temporarily receded, but he maintained his concern with the form through his essays on specific authors and works and on general problems of literature.

As a prolific literary journalist, Borges, from the 1920s onward, frequently drew attention to the work of short story writers, attempting to broaden the range of tastes of the Argentine reading public. A great many readers of short fiction were conversant with Spanish- and French-language currents in this form. This readership still admired the sumptuous, sensuous prose popularized by the turn-of-the-century modernist movement. Also in vogue was the "cold," or "cruel," story tendency exemplified by such masters as Guy de Maupassant and his popular contemporary Jules Amédée Barbey d'Aurevilly. This was the era when two masters of the hair-raising tale, the Argentine Leopoldo Lugones and the Uruguayan-born Horacio Quiroga, were powerful presences in Buenos Aires literary life. Borges disparaged the luxuriant descriptive prose of modernism. But he concurred, to a considerable extent, with the popular tendency to favor narratives with paradoxical and ironic twists of fate, mental and physical violence, and frequent recourse to fantastic, or at least eerie, elements. His literary commentary, though, encouraged readers to go beyond established patterns and sample the work of writers from other literary cultures and traditions.

Borges had a lifelong practice of championing writers whose stories might at first be hard to appreciate because of their idiosyncrasy, as in the case of one of his own unusual tastes, Chesterton. He vigorously promoted the tale of detection and the science fiction story. In his far-ranging readings, he developed special enthusiasms for some non-Western forms of brief narrative. *A Thousand and One Nights* especially fascinated him, both in itself and for the paradoxes of its reception by readers outside the Arabic cultural sphere. Though itself a cycle of poems, *The Rubáiyát of Omar Khayyám*, in Edward FitzGerald's well-known English version, became an important point of reference for Borges's prose. He came to understand the curious phenomenon of its English version as a parable of the involuntary and mysterious nature of creation; translation had produced a work unlike, and more memorable than, anything written individually by either Khayyám or FitzGerald. In addition, Borges admired the poems for their eloquent assertion of the relativism of truths. (Many readers have been struck by the resemblances between the concepts central to the *Rubáiyát* and the recurring ideas in *Ficciones* and *The Aleph*.) He also prized Asian and Arabic parables and fables, admiring the way they avoided overt statement by relying on cryptically significant objects, such as birds and jewels.

Borges learned from Islamic and Far Eastern models in developing the now-famous repertory of symbolically meaningful tokens that recur in his stories: labyrinths, swords, coins and other small round objects, mirrors, moons, chessboards, masks, roses, maps, tigers, towers, books, and many others. In addition, Borges utilized the Arabic and Asian worlds as backdrops for a great deal of his short fiction. It should be pointed out, though, that his relations with oriental sources were more remote than his ties to Germanic languages and literatures. Borges had native familiarity with English and was a proficient reader of German. In Scandinavian linguistic and cultural matters, Borges's enthusiasm at times ran ahead of his knowledge, but he sought expertise; he struggled to become a learned commentator on the system of Icelandic verse and on occasion determined to learn Old Norse. His Eastern material, in contrast, came to him in translation and without much contextualizing information about the source cultures. Though Borges sometimes regretted the more significant gaps in his knowledge, such as his ignorance of Semitic languages, he did not mind using vaguely grasped cultures as a simple backdrop for his stories. In other words, he could be an unabashed exoticist.

Borges's relations to his Jewish source material are more complex than his orientalism. He knew a fair amount about certain issues, such as the philosophical thought of Baruch Spinoza and some aspects of cabala, but his knowledge was always that of an enthusiast rather than of someone seeking uniform coverage of a topic. Borges liked to mention the possibility of Jewish forebears in his genealogy, partly to give pause to Argentine anti-Semites and partly to remind readers of the long-denied Jewish element in Spanish- and Portuguese-language cultures. His passionate but erratic explorations of Jewish learning are well documented in Aizenberg's earlier cited work, while studies by Jaime Alazraki, the longtime Borges scholar, Saúl Sosnowski and others focus on the author's use of cabalistic concepts.[4]

While Borges's choice of works to praise was at times unpredictable, his general criteria of judgment were easily discernible. A frankly artificial literary construction, such as the framing story of *A Thousand and One Nights*, struck Borges as more stimulating and provocative than any realistic presentation. Borges considered it a pointless falsification to try to make art seem lifelike and natural; undisguised artifice was more truthful. Borges praised realistic writers only when, in his judgment, they went beyond verisimilitude. He was insistent in favoring stories relying on symbol and allegory. Borges admired writers who could perform well in this mode whether they drew on conventional literary symbology or, as in the case of experimental modern authors, developed their own variant forms. Borges's own short stories exhibit a mixture of traditional emblems and tokens with symbols from his own idiosyncratic system.

As well as the reviewing of books, Borges's journalistic work included the elaboration of local-color pieces, in many cases describing the city's small-time underworld. These were sketches rather than short stories, but provided a point of departure toward fiction; Borges's first work of brief fiction, "El hombre de la esquina rosada" ("Streetcorner Man"), was a reworking of one of these vignettes.

Borges also offered his readers stories that were not of his own invention but appeared in his rendering—his translation or summary of the basic anecdote. In 1933, Borges began to edit the Saturday arts-and-entertainment supplement of the newspaper *Crítica* (Criticism); the job, though not pursued continuously over a lengthy stretch, required him to generate a good deal of material for this publication. During 1936–39, he had a more inescapable writing task: the responsibility for filling the literary page of a women's magazine, *El hogar* (Home). Here he gained considerable experience as a secondhand narrator, translating and reworking unusual narratives culled from his wide-ranging readings. Borges, then as later, had a special knack for retelling plots, summarizing other people's narratives so as best to display the features that aroused his enthusiasm.

These activities, though carried out with unusual spirit, belong to a period, stretching from the 1920s well into the 1930s, when Borges, simply needing gainful employment, produced a good deal of ephemeral reading matter. Rodríguez Monegal (306) notes that the stints at *Crítica* and *El hogar* were far from being the lowest point of Borges's years on Grub Street. These jobs did, however, provide him with a stock of themes and narrative strategies on which he could draw as he began to shift his own prose gradually toward the short fiction form. The work published in *Crítica* was itself strong enough to provide the material for a book-length collection, the 1935 *Historia universal de la infamia* (*A Universal History of Infamy*, 1972). Mary Lusky Friedman has examined Borges's refashioning of his work for newspapers and magazines as part of his move toward fiction.[5] Among elements easily recognizable to readers of Borges's well-known fiction is the situation whereby someone not directly connected with the original summarizes a narrative or reference work.

During this transitional period, Borges was an active but not a major figure on the Buenos Aires literary scene, as he had been ever since he won attention as the founding figure of the city's avant-garde movement. He had an important supporter in Victoria Ocampo (1891–1979), whose influence had grown especially great since the 1931 founding of her literary magazine *Sur* (South). Ocampo was particularly eager to promote authors who worked well in nonrealistic modes; she favored highly imaginative writing and the element of the "cosmopolitan," to use the contemporary byword. Herself anxious to influence public tastes in literature, Ocampo appreciated Borges's efforts to shape the reading habits of the Argentine public. His knowledge of and enthusiasm for English- and German-language literatures and his ability to draw on non-Western sources made him an unusual asset for a publication determined to be cosmopolitan.

With *Sur* as a showcase for his book reviews, Borges began to experiment with the form. Many of Borges's reviews are really "about" something other than the books under discussion and need to be read as one would read original, creative work. At times, his cryptic, elliptical offerings appear to be commenting principally on their own unusual style and construction and on the way in which they are likely to be read. Reading and writing then become Borges's chief preoccupations, displacing the authors and works that are normally the primary focus of book reviews. Borges had mastered the conventions of many forms of writing and often experimented with a purposeful confusion of genres. One of the most famous of Borges's devices, harkening back to his tenure at *Sur*, would be the short story that purported to be a book review or essay. Borges's fictional reviewers quickly prove to be troubled characters with more on their minds than the performance of their literary-journalistic tasks. Borges could write a straightforward, informative review, however, when his point was to present an author worthy of attention. For example, when he became the Argentine discoverer of Franz Kafka's short fiction (his interest in the Prague writer's novels remained limited); he published, in August 1937, a general introduction written as plainly as a textbook.

Sur was not simply a magazine; it also published books and served as a central liaison for many types of literary activities, such as the coordination of lecture tours for visiting writers and the bringing together of authors, critics, and translators. Borges, who was generally adept in the world of letters, became involved in a number of *Sur*-related undertakings. He carried out translations commissioned by the magazine, including two works by Virginia Woolf, *A Room of One's Own* (a selection of essays published under the English title in 1936) and *Orlando*.

Moving in these circles, Borges developed friendly and collegial relations with the novelist and short story writer Adolfo Bioy Casares (b. 1914), who would be his collaborator on apparently lighthearted, but bitingly satirical, brief fiction. Bioy would also achieve an unusual international fame as a character in several of Borges's short stories. Most famously, in "Tlön, Uqbar, Orbis Tertius," the fictional Bioy speculates with the narrator on the possibility of encoding disturbing knowledge in a narrative, then brings him a book that destroys his world. Silvina Ocampo (Victoria's sister, b. 1906), who would distinguish herself as the author of fantastic short stories, joined Borges and Bioy in lengthy discussions of inventive fiction. They argued the merits of texts already written and conjectured about possible new ones. Their shared enthusiasm for this form and eagerness to champion it against realistic fiction culminated in the much-reprinted *Antología de la literatura fantástica* (*The Book of Fantasy*, 1989). The three friends' selection of tightly constructed, nonrealistic stories appeared in 1940, the same year Bioy and Silvina Ocampo were married, with Borges as witness. This collection strengthened the Argentine public's taste for artfully fashioned, nonrealistic short fiction. At least equally important, working and conversing with these two friends helped Borges to develop the concepts that would shape his fiction.

A *Universal History of Infamy*

With the 1935 publication of *Historia universal de la infamia* (*A Universal History of Infamy*, 1970), Borges moved toward the short story in two ways.[6] This collection of retold accounts of spectacular and remorseless villainy, written originally for *Crítica*, included an unexpected extra: "Hombre de la esquina rosada" ("Streetcorner Man"), which is definitely a short story. It employs material that Borges had used in the 1920s but does so as a "factual" local-color sketch, in the mode of an observer's notes on the city's lowlife (Friedman, 59). In 1933 he published in *Crítica* the version that is now generally counted as his first short story to see print. For example, Rodríguez Monegal is referring to the appearance of this reworked version when he asserts that "Borges had been writing fiction at least since 1933" (324). The publication in *Crítica* was under the pseudonym H. Bustos, a circumstance Stabb (90) cites as further evidence of Borges's longtime fear of presenting himself as a short story writer.

The narrator of "Streetcorner Man," a minor gang member, leads the reader up to a single emblematic fictional event, an episode in which a man idolized for his toughness suddenly appears to lose his physical courage. The rest of the story then reports the consequences of this disturbing lapse, with the last line throwing new light on the events. It is this reworking, which Borges himself would later recognize as fully a short story (Friedman, 69), that the author included in his 1935 collection, giving it its definitive, memorable title. While it cannot give any idea of the intricate, paradoxical qualities of Borges's most highly esteemed stories, "Streetcorner Man" does present two distinctive elements that recur sporadically throughout Borges's fiction-writing career. One is the view of gang life through the eyes of a low-ranking member who watches, with first admiration and then disillusionment, the activities of a dominant figure. Another is the moment when bodily courage will either manifest itself or prove shamefully lacking.

While this account of a street lord's downfall announces Borges's new willingness to enter the genre, its straightforwardness and simplicity do not give a very accurate vision of the characteristic shape the author's short fiction would assume. For an insight into the distinctive form Borges was developing, one should examine instead the narratives that compose the bulk of the 1935 work, all presented as essays about infamous behavior. The characteristic that bears close attention is their ambiguous kinship with the short story.

A useful question to consider is what distinguishes these brief narratives from the short story as modern readers expect to find it. It is true that Borges based these accounts on sources that at least claimed to be factual; the collection includes an appendix citing sources. To a limited extent, rooting the stories in fact separates them from purely imaginative writing. This criterion, though, is not as significant as it might seem. Imaginative writing often takes real-world occurrences as its point of departure, and Borges was imaginative indeed in his free adaptation of his source accounts.

A more important trait pushes these essays toward the border of the short story, although it does not make them seem altogether at home in the genre. This feature is the idiosyncratic character of the narrator. The difference between expository and imaginative writing, according to a commonsense tradition going back to classical antiquity, is that in the former, the voice that speaks is that of the author himself. The narrator of the tales of infamy is not explicitly identified as anyone other than Borges, but he is a stagily exaggerated persona the author has developed to tell these particular stories. A specialist in the evil behavior of human beings, he is oddly unconcerned with ethical issues, an attitude shared by the amoral villains he describes. While morality leaves him indifferent, the style with which his subjects carry out their misdeeds fascinates him; again, the same outlook contaminates the infamous characters, who take great pains to be criminal with a show of nonchalant flair. The narrator has his attention equally focused upon the mannered fashion in which he relates his stories, filling them with self-conscious asides and features that draw readers' notice to matters of literary language and narrative construction. Manner and mannerisms continually upstage and predominate over the meanings to be extracted from the episodes. This emphasis on the elaboration of crime and crime stories is always attributable to the whimsical narrator, with his habit of striking poses. There are frequent reminders that the narrator is acting capriciously: he barely notes matters with serious ethical implications, but lavishes baroque description on details that engage him aesthetically. The evidence of his irresponsibility further separates him from the real-life Borges, who was a veteran practitioner of literary composition and sure of how to produce a traditionally well-made narrative—when that was what he cared to achieve.

In situating the accounts of infamy almost, but not quite, in the terrain of the short story, Borges used a device that would become a famous element in his repertory: narrators who parade an erudition that turns out to be spurious. Scholarly treatises and reference works are cited with an assured air of knowledgeability, but many of them turn out to have no existence outside Borges's sphere of invention. "El tintorero enmascarado, Hákkim de Merv" ("The Masked Dyer, Hákkim of Merv"), for example, begins with the chronicler citing the four principal sources of information about the duplicitous protagonist and his career of imposture. All four are fictitious (Friedman, 67). In other instances, Borges would comment on books he had invented for just that purpose, using the book review format as a starting point for what would reveal itself as a work of fiction. In another variant, allusions to real texts arouse distrust when surrounded by elements clearly concocted for the fictional occasion. In learning to deal with Borges's stories, readers come to suspect all references either of being outright inventions or of making misleading use of an extant work.

While all the accounts of infamy have some fictional features, certain of them are particularly close to Borges's short stories. "The Masked Dyer," the most inventive of these narratives, prefigures some of Borges's recurrent thematic concerns. Treachery and deceit are rife in the world of Borges's stories; the Masked Dyer is a false prophet who misleads an entire sect. Although some aspects of the account are ludicrous, the stripping away of Hákkim's mask to reveal a leprous rather than a divinely luminous face is a charged moment. "The Masked Dyer" can, like many of Borges's stories, be understood as a cautionary tale about the human desire for transcendental knowledge. The Masked Dyer operates by seeming to possess an absolute truth that illuminates him from within, but the revelation of his secret is disgusting and trivial rather than enlightening and ennobling. Another typical Borges note appears in the veiled prophet's resemblance to an artist. Both his original occupation—applying colors to naturally drab cloth—and his new role as a fabulous prophet wearing a beautiful mask identify him as a maker of artifices. The analogy between the impostor and the artist is one of Borges's many reminders to readers that art is necessarily pretense, not truth telling in any direct way.

"El impostor inverosímil Tom Castro" ("Tom Castro, the Implausible Impostor") is constructed around a central paradox. Taking advantage of the uncertainty surrounding reports of disasters, Castro impersonates a wealthy man who has died at sea. He presents himself, ready to assume the dead man's place in life, without altering his appearance or personal habits. His mentor and partner in crime has guessed that those who know the missing man would be most suspicious of a replica or simulacrum, whose divergences from the original would reveal themselves by contrasting with memories. The least suspect replacement would be a person so radically different as to allow no ground for comparison. An allegory of art suggests itself; realism is less effective than stylization. While the former must compete with the real world and can be checked against it and faulted for discrepancies, the latter can establish an autonomous realm.

"Tom Castro" is not only an abstractly symbolic narrative but also an excellent early example of Borges's persistent implication that concepts commonly relied upon to make sense of the world are arbitrary and fragile. The narrator cites particular reasons that the imposture succeeds: the dead man's mother is determined that he be alive; she first sees Castro in a glaring light. These factors, though, cannot account for the acceptance Castro enjoys until his mentor's death, unless one admits that strictly individualized human identity is not a naturally robust and self-evident form of truth. The mentor understands that self-serving human beings establish what is true, and makes it in people's interest to agree that Castro is the heir. The ease with which one identity can be stretched to cover two dissimilar bodies and types of behavior suggests that identity itself may be elastic and transferable. Many of Borges's later stories advance this notion more strongly by making the point that two characters in essence share one identity, or that an apparently individual figure contains traces of many people.

A Universal History of Infamy also contains abundant samples of Borges's gift for describing ruin, shabbiness, and squalor. The setting of "El espantoso redentor Lazarus Morell" ("The Dread Redeemer Lazarus Morell") is the Mississippi Delta. The narrator, displaying his fondness for excess, provides copious and luridly overstated descriptions of the geography and population of the area. The Mississippi River is singled out for its relentless discharge of sludge, accretions, and debris into the Gulf of Mexico; the lands it drains, in its sluggish way, are waterlogged and pestilent. Mimicking an old-fashioned deterministic social scientist, the narrator asserts that inhabitants of the sodden, clogged delta are enfeebled in body and decadent in their social organization. The pseudoscientific characterization of local geography and society turns out to be comically inefficacious in explaining Morell's misdeeds. Villainy remains an enigma beyond accounting through such ostensibly objective factors as environment and heredity.

"El asesino desinteresado Bill Harrigan" ("The Disinterested Killer Bill Harrigan"), in telling the tale of Billy the Kid, brings out the curiously hermetic, remote quality that distinguishes the infamy of these accounts. Billy the Kid, as the title notes, has no specifiable motive for killing at least twenty-one persons. The narrator hints that Billy is a variant of the fanatical ascetic. As his crimes and his evil reputation exclude Billy from the society of his fellow beings, he achieves a form of purity through detachment, almost uncontaminated by human ties or even by the meager luxury of a place of residence. Support for the interpretation of the story as a tale of self-mortification and questing comes from the descriptions of the wild West. This no-man's-land appears either as a comfortless landscape across which Billy is impelled or else as haphazard settlements of disaffected outsiders.

In a move typical of Borges, concern has been shifted away from the examination of crime as a social phenomenon. Billy is unmistakably a sociopath and frontier society a setting propitious to his type of behavior. Still, these reflections of social reality are drained of significance. Throughout his career, Borges would be subject to criticism for his habit of using subject matter with evident social implications while omitting from his treatment the consideration of society.

"La viuda Ching, pirata puntual" ("The Widow Ching, Lady Pirate") has a comically lengthy opening section in which the narrator delays launching into his main topic by citing various cases of female pirates. While this extended prefatory material is jocular and sprightly, the story of the widow Ching unfolds with greater sobriety. The narrator draws appreciative attention to the graceful, elegant touches that characterize Ching's career in crime and ends with a tale of persuasion through allegory. While all the accounts feature criminals concerned with show and panache, Ching goes the furthest in her attention to aesthetic detail, making her pirate ship a work of calculated beauty. The emperor who convinces her to abandon her operations does so by using an equally elaborate presentation. He sends her a succession of kites, each bearing the same message encoded in a fable, until his urgings for her to place herself under his protection finally prove cumulatively effective.

"El incivil maestro de ceremonias Kotsuké no Suké" ("The Insulting Master of Etiquette Kotsuké no Suké") is, in comparison to the earlier described accounts, more of a retelling than an inventive undertaking on Borges's part. Its plot is the celebrated Japanese legend of the Forty-seven Ronian. In rendering it in Spanish, Borges highlights those aspects which might strike a non-Asian reader as strange, such as the importance placed on losing and saving face and the rituals surrounding honor suicide. Though Borges mastered considerable knowledge of other cultures and could be urbane and cosmopolitan when he cared to, there is no doubt he also savored the childish notion that foreigners are incomprehensibly alien, along with the effects to be obtained when the narrator of a text takes this unsophisticated view. Borges's treatment of the Japanese legend is also noteworthy for its emphasis on paradox; his title is not very representative of the contents of the story, but does call attention to a dramatic contradiction occurring early in the tale.

"El proveedor de iniquidades Monk Eastman" ("Monk Eastman, Purveyor of Iniquities") has as its setting the New York underworld. Here Borges has done relatively little to rework his material into narrative form, remaining for the most part within the limits of the local-color vignette. As in many of his treatments of the analogous sector of Buenos Aires society, Borges concerns himself with the legends surrounding celebrated gangsters. The emphasis is not on criminals able to build empires, amass fortunes, or exercise widespread control, but on those who go about their business with the greatest display of personal distinction and flair. Eastman meets this criterion with the flashy cruelty with which he and his men intimidate rival gang members. In fanciful contrast is the openhearted good nature Eastman reserves for the many cats with whom he develops an extraordinary bond.

Critical attention to the stories of *A Universal History of Infamy* was slow in coming and has remained sporadic. There is a tendency to regard these accounts as belonging to the long process of development leading up to Borges's mature fiction, principally of concern for what they reveal about the author's thematic preoccupations and notions of literary language and narrative construction. Still, occasional criticism treats these works as being of autonomous interest. The Infamy stories were unexpectedly placed in the spotlight when the internationally regarded critic and literary theorist Paul de Man praised their highly stylized aspect in "A Modern Master."[7] This essay, published in the 19 November 1954 *New York Review of Books*, appeared when Borges was still little known in the United States and Britain. De Man was, for the most part, presenting him to new readers. This general introduction gave surprising prominence to *A Universal History of Infamy*, which at that time was not even available in English. De Man is struck by the way the texts maintain style, particularly their own, in the foreground. In his analysis, writing that is about style and narrative that is centered on acts of infamy—especially notable in *A Universal History of Infamy*—are hallmarks of all Borges's fiction. De Man accords the collection equal standing with the famous later short stories collected in *Ficciones* and *The Aleph*. In this respect, De Man's observations represent a minority point of view among Borges critics.

Although there has been an upsurge in the frequency with which the 1935 collection attracts commentary, there is no doubt that most critics do not classify it among Borges's short fiction (with the exception of "Streetcorner Man") or consider it of great scholarly interest except in relation to the author's later work. It is viewed, above all, as testimony to the early development or prehistory of the form that would become the Borges short story. An especially detailed inquiry along these lines is the chapter "Origins of the Paradigm: *A Universal History of Infamy*" in Friedman's *The Emperor's Kites: A Morphology of Borges' Tales* (55–108). Friedman is concerned with the development of a single type of tale that she finds repeated throughout Borges's work and considers, among other things, a disguised expression of grief. The texts of *Infamy* attract her attention because they predate the stories that give an altogether literary form to Borges's recurring concerns and to the event—the death of the author's father—that Friedman sees as stimulating the full emergence of "the Borgean tale." Alazraki, the critic who has most fully explored the stylistic aspects of Borges's work, takes an interest in *Infamy* for what it reveals of "The Making of a Style."[8] Later, Borges, reviewing this period of his career, would often refer to his earlier self as a timid writer, stricken with shyness at the thought of entering the serious literary genre of the short story. The short sketches of villains were baroque games he invented, procrastinating to avoid the real work of composing short stories. He refers to the *Infamy* texts in typically disparaging terms in the interview with Fernando Sorrentino excerpted in Part 2 of this volume.

Yet as "Streetcorner Man" had demonstrated, Borges was already able to produce a short story well within the contemporary conventions of the genre. Besides, he had not appeared intimidated by the equally prestigious form of lyrical poetry and had a considerable history of risk taking in his writing. The problem he was struggling with was surely not how to dare to write a short story, or even how to perform adequately in the genre. Instead, the difficulty that prompted the anomalous tales of infamy would seem to be that of going beyond what had already been done in the short story and developing a form that would bear

Borges's individual mark. Probably the feature most often cited as distinguishing Borges's short fiction is the inclusion of elements that strike readers as more typical of expository prose. Borges's specialties include the short story presented as if it were a report, study, summary of findings, or critical essay; the person presenting the account then turns out to be a fictional construct and the events recounted are further inventions. Even when the story does not assume the format of a mock document, certain elements appear that are reminiscent of nonfiction: erudite-sounding asides or passages in which a speaker who seems to be Borges gives his analysis of the events just narrated and their meaning. Even when narrative clearly predominates, the stories may remind readers of the essay by focusing attention on issues long debated in this form, as certain perennial questions of philosophy.

The next book-length collection of Borges's work was, on the whole, less ambiguous in its generic identity; the 1936 *Historia de la eternidad* (History of eternity) consisted principally of essays on two of Borges's great themes. One of these topics is the diverse ways in which time, and timelessness, may be conceptualized and symbolically represented. Borges was eager to remind readers that the notion of a steadily progressing time was only one of many possible chronological systems. His other focus in this work is the transformations that literary and philosophical writings undergo as they are understood, interpreted, and translated; an important subcategory is the ethnocentric coloration that writers impart to their portraits of foreign cultures.

A book of essays, this work contains "El acercamiento a Almotásim" ("The Approach to al-Mu'tasim").[9] "Approach to al-Mu'tasim" is another experiment in the complexities that can result when a literary invention presents itself as if it were a nonfiction account, typically one rendered at second- or thirdhand from sources that may be of dubious reliability. This text, first published as one of a series of essays, was reclassified when Borges, having finally acknowledged himself as a story writer, reprinted it in his first collection of short fiction, the 1941 *El jardín de senderos que se bifurcan* (*The Garden of Forking Paths*, a book title Borges abandoned in favor of *Ficciones* when he published the much-expanded edition of 1944, of which the 1941 collection composes a subsection). While in the discussion of Borges's work it is common to speak of the tales of infamy as nearly or virtually short stories, "Approach to al-Mu'tasim" is unreservedly assigned to this category. With its appearance, the characteristic Borges story has fully emerged.

"Approach to al-Mu'tasim" begins as if it were a book review by a literary journalist routinely performing his duties. The job of characterizing a (fictitious) detective novel soon loses interest for the reviewer, who instead becomes absorbed by an extraordinary sequence of events contained in the plot. The entire chain of occurrences begins with a seemingly modern, secularized law student becoming inexplicably drawn into Moslem-Hindu sectarian violence, hiding from the authorities among the untouchables and seeking out first a woman of the thieving class and then al-Mu'tasim, the source of radiance in the world.

The young man's pilgrimage toward some pure truth leads him through degrading circumstances. The night he is transformed from a secular rationalist into a devout pilgrim, a dirty corpse robber he finds urinating in the open air serves as his guide and mentor. The pilgrim eventually locates the glow and hears "the unimaginable voice of al-Mu'tasim" (English *Ficciones* 49; Spanish *Ficciones* 40), pulls open a curtain, and advances to meet him—at which point the novel ends, although the reviewer has some further commentary.

The novel's cryptic ending suggests that the student has found what is for him a satisfactory revelation. There is, however, no assurance that the result is knowledge. It is possible to conclude, based on hints contained in the story, that the student is destroyed or transformed by his vision and that he earns a glimpse either of nothingness or of plenitude. Carter Wheelock, in his 1969 *The Mythmaker: A Study of Motif and Symbol in the Short Stories of Jorge Luis Borges*, interprets the ending as consistent with a pattern he traces in all the stories of Borges's high period. He concludes that the seeker has discovered "the completed abstraction . . . of a reality which the student has chosen to elevate to momentary supremacy"—that is, the absolute goodness that has come to obsess him.[10] Some element of self-encounter must necessarily be figured into any account of this absolute vision, for a footnote offers a fable whose moral is that the sought-after other is oneself. In the closing remarks is the suggestion that al-Mu'tasim is in quest of another, who is looking for yet a further figure of perfection, and so on in an infinite regression. For all these leads, the nature of the revelatory experience remains an X factor.

An aggressive skeptic might discount the quest as a worthless undertaking, begun by accident and continued on the ingenuous presupposition that a human being can gain definitive possession of the most profoundly significant knowledge. But such a reading fails to take into account some of the evidence in this equivocal text. There are clues that the pilgrim deserves some respect. He is eager to listen and learn, and mysterious symbols, such as circular forms, recur throughout his quest and suggest that magical forces accompany him. The worth of locating al-Mu'tasim can never be either established or disproved.

Such all-absorbing inquiries whose value remains uncertain figure in many Borges stories. They include fieldwork, expeditions, and fact-finding missions; research in libraries and archives and attempts to trace elusive works and references; scrutiny of photographs, illustrations, maps, and other visual evidence; consultation of reference works and the pronouncements of authorities; divination and magic; cryptography, decipherment, and translation; and the pursuit of a line of philosophical or theological thought to its ultimate consequences. Whatever the method, the outcome is always less, and sometimes much less, than a definitive triumph over ignorance.

The chronicler who reports on the accidental and perhaps misdirected seeker of al-Mu'tasim is a typical Borges narrator in another important way. He puts himself forward as one concerned with relaying information, specifically the contents of a book assigned him for review. But the way he goes about presenting this information is, to use a word often applied to Borges's stories, bewildering. Although he presumably has access to the novel under discussion, he is frequently vacillating and uncertain in his description of its contents. Like many Borges narrators, he at times has a mastery of odd details but is missing what would seem to be basic pieces of information. His narrative is full of indications of uncertainty, such as giving two alternative possibilities for a single point of fact. His problem is more deeply seated than the mechanical difficulty of summarizing a detective novel that turns out to be a cryptic allegory: the narrator's mind is suffering a type of paralysis. He is at a loss to absorb the mass of narrative data and to organize it well enough to communicate it to others.

His poor ability to grasp and synthesize information magnifies the confusion inherent in the situation of the pilgrim, who wanders unwittingly through events of unclear significance. When readers speak of a story or, by extension, a real-life situation as being "Borgean," they most typically refer to a perception that matters are becoming too intricate and unwieldy to make sense of. Protagonists, narrators, and readers of Borges's stories are frequently overwhelmed by proliferating data that disarm their mental faculties.

After producing this universe of confusion, this sense of overload, Borges's stories often show, in contrast, the relief the human mind finds in systems of belief and thought. These order-bringing systems cause their adherents either to focus their thoughts narrowly or to attempt to take in unlimited knowledge all at once—a pair of reciprocal tendencies that will be discussed in more detail in relation to Borges's most famous short stories. In either case, systems are strongly associated (whether as cause or result is an ambiguous point) with the revelation of unquestionable truths and of an absolute overall design to the universe. Yet such cosmic glimpses, initially welcomed for their patterning effect, may prove equivocal, arbitrary, and inconsistent. In the worst cases, excessive zeal to possess truth, revelations, and solid beliefs destroys certain of Borges's characters. Others are merely subjected to disillusionment, and may later reject what they have experienced while in the grip of a doctrine or mystical perception. Still another set of protagonists can be distinguished: these last seem satisfied with the new perspective obtained in a visionary moment, but their discoveries remain opaque to the reader, who cannot see why they are valuable. In one case, "La busca de Averroes" ("Averroes's Search") from *The Aleph*, the protagonist is pleased with a suddenly revealed insight that both narrator and reader know to be defective. The form of mystic vision most rarely seen in Borges is one that actually uplifts the individual affected. The most positive case occurs in "Historia del guerrero y de la cautiva" ("Story of the Warrior and the Captive"), in *The Aleph*. Here the warrior's glimpse of a greater order is an improving experience; readers can see the effects of inspiration, but are left uncertain what the character learned in the instant of illumination.

In a number of Borges's stories, protagonists remain satisfied with the beliefs they have acquired, but readers, as they progress through the tale, have less and less reason to see these mental constructs as worthwhile. Such doubt is especially acute when the character's special knowledge or vision is summarized in the text (often the narrative breaks off just when such a revelation is imminent). The summary nearly always contains some clue that the information is flawed. What the protagonist sees and knows may seem inherently absurd, pointless, or misconceived, or its meaning may be opaque to readers.

Having developed all the basic elements of his typical form of brief fiction, Borges still hesitated to consider himself a short story writer or to take the logical next step of publishing a collection of work in this genre. His own account of this blockage and how he overcame it is itself a symbolically weighted and often-told tale, which receives its most literary elaboration in "An Autobiographical Essay" (*The Aleph and Other Stories*, 203–60). Borges reworks the raw material of his life; discrepancies between this version and biographical data are easily identified. These obvious modifications of the life story have given rise to psychoanalytic interpretations by Rodríguez Monegal (323–26) and Friedman (156–57). Of most interest for the present discussion is Borges's statement that, in 1939, he had "never really" written a short story (*The Aleph and Other Stories*, 243). Yet as I've already noted, "Streetcorner Man" was published in *Crítica* in 1933 and collected in *A Universal History of Infamy* in 1935, while "The Approach to al-Mu'tasim" appeared in Borges's 1936 collection of philosophical essays.

In Borges's "Autobiographical Essay" he was only able to emerge as a short story writer after a near-death experience (he developed blood poisoning following an injury late in 1938). During his recovery, Borges feared he would never again have the "mental integrity" to read and write. Reasoning that "if I tried something I had never really done before and failed at that, it wouldn't be so bad, and might even prepare me for the final revelation," Borges says, "I decided I would try to write a story" (*The Aleph and Other Stories*, 243). After this resolution, he wrote "Pierre Menard, autor del Quijote" ("Pierre Menard, Author of *Don Quixote*" in Anthony Bonner's translation in *Ficciones*; "Pierre Menard, Author of the *Quixote*" in James E. Irby's version included in *Labyrinths*), one of the most frequently and divergently interpreted of his stories.

Borges's "Autobiographical Essay" can be taken not as literal information but as an expression of his anxiety at becoming the author of short fiction. As Stabb notes, "he had on several occasions expressed the idea that he viewed the genre as forbidden territory" (91). There was some cause for trepidation, as before any difficult and consuming undertaking. And yet despite his initial hesitation, Borges would become absorbed in—and largely indentified with—his work as a short story writer and would make significant, complex innovations in the genre.

Ficciones

Between 1939 and the early 1950s Borges produced a succession of short stories, many of which are now widely known and draw continuing critical attention. These are the texts of the 1944 *Ficciones* (the eight stories of the 1942 collection and six more) and the 1949 *El Aleph*, together with five stories added to the 1952 edition of *El Aleph* and three to the 1956 *Ficciones*. The 1956 collection includes no work produced subsequent to, at the latest, 1954. The year 1954, then, marks the end of Borges's major period of short story production and the beginning of some dozen years of apparent abstention from this form.[11]

The very titles of the two collections achieved a kind of celebrity; both became shorthand terms of reference for aspects of Borges's story writing. The Aleph, a small sphere permitting all aspects of the universe to be seen simultaneously, is the object of a quest by one of Borges's truth seekers. It has come to emblematize the illusion of an objectively existing totality of absolute knowledge that human beings can possess. *Ficciones* (fictions) is a term sometimes used to refer to Borges's stories of the major period because these texts call attention to their own fictiveness. They contain reminders that they are only pretending to open a window through which readers may observe the truth about phenomena. Their boldly flaunted status is that of invented, constructed, and possibly falsified artifacts, a status they attribute also to other results of artistic and intellectual endeavor. Consistent with the frank admission that fiction is artifice is the emphasis on the literary devices employed. The artistic decisions that determine style, the selection of a type of narrator, and the use of framing devices and allusions to symbolic objects, among other technical elements, all stand out clearly. The story is not meant to seem natural, an effect Borges regarded as an impoverishment of fiction's possibilities and a falsification of its artistic character. Rather, fictional narrative should reveal itself as something designed and fabricated, the result of deliberate choices among conventions.

From these two collections, another catchword emerges: *labyrinths*, a word that has served as the title of the Greek and Norwegian translations of *Ficciones* and of French, English, German, and Spanish anthologies of Borges selections. The word is one Borges frequently used in the titles and texts of his stories, although never to name a book. He made a hobby of collecting myths and folklore about these puzzling constructions; an attentive reader of Borges can glean a good amount of information about the building and navigation of labyrinths. Borges's concern with structures designed to entrap and disorient clearly arises from the need for a metaphor for orders, systems, or worlds overwhelming in their complexity and ambiguity. In his stories, not only mazes but also buildings, cities, terrain, waterways, and vegetation reveal sinisterly labyrinthine aspects. The labyrinth is also metaphorically representative of such abstractions as destiny, time, and space, as well as of such human productions as music, games, warfare, literature, religion, and philosophy. The human body and mind, together with the universe as registered by the mind, are shown as inherently mazelike. Borges's readers have been quick to identify his stories as another of the forms the labyrinth assumes.

Many other typical traits recur in these famous stories, fascinating Borges aficionados and giving rise to parodies. The first-person narrator frequently bears the name Borges and often shares many characteristics of the real-world author. The Borges of the stories receives no favored treatment, though, and indeed is apt to exemplify such human weaknesses as petty rivalry, long-festering resentment, and shyness. Borges sets an occasional phrase or sentence in English in the midst, or as the title, of a Spanish-language story. His protagonists often find themselves in red enclosures, a feature giving rise to Freudian speculation. The bibliophile Borges often includes detailed information on the style of type, pagination, or other identifying characteristics of a fictional text. His narrators at times pause to note typical features of the older architecture of Buenos Aires and its environs. A specialty of Borges's is the portrayal of deterioration: dismantled houses, ruined buildings and monuments, gardens run wild, the remains of abandoned projects, shabby neighborhoods, and entire regions fallen into neglect. Chess and *truco* (a popular Argentine card game) are prominent among the exercises in chance, strategy, and divination undertaken in Borges stories.

Secret societies and conspiracies are another favored element, as are utopian schemes to remold human language. There is a frequent emphasis on groups capable of commanding loyalty, especially nationalities and ethnicities. Of these, Borges seems unusually fascinated with the private collectivity composed of the members of his own family, including its ancestors. He is also concerned with four more publicly recognized particularities: Jews, Arabs, Scandinavians, and Chinese, each at various times reputed to be tightly knit and aware of belonging to a subgroup. Borges's ancestors and representatives of these four ethnic categories show up time and again in his famous stories. (In the lesser known tales of his late period, Celts and Norsemen are preeminent.) Another sign of the author's preoccupation with tribes or clans is the construction of fictional names from an international mixture of components, the Germanic languages providing most of the lexical stock.

While all these features are subject to purely literary interpretation, it is difficult to escape the idea that they also reflect Borges's personal obsessions, predilections, and anxieties. This notion would seem to underlie the common practice of referring to "the Borgean universe." The phrase suggests that, whether their backdrop is the Arab countries, the streets of Buenos Aires, or some other scenario, the fictions occur in an autonomous world dominated down to the last of its numerous details by the mind of Jorge Luis Borges.

"Tlön, Uqbar, Orbis Tertius" is the lead story in *Ficciones* and among the quintessential Borges narratives. As well as the usual audience for Borges's stories, "Tlön" has attracted a second readership among enthusiasts of science fiction: witness its occasional inclusion in anthologies of stories in this subgenre. Its kinship to science fiction lies in its use, as a point of departure, of the notion of alternate worlds. It is typical in its inclusion of a narrator who represents Borges. Although here the name Borges does not appear (in many of these stories the narrator is a namesake of the author's), names of several of Borges's real-life friends do, and other features of the narrator-protagonist coincide with those of the real-life author. Also characteristically, the story is presented as a report, beginning with a detailed discussion of the bibliographic sources that have supposedly led Borges to the topic. As is often the case, the supporting research evidence is flawed. The trail begins with an unauthorized reissue of the *Encyclopaedia Britannica*, cited by Bioy Casares in a conversation with Borges. This work contains information on a place called Uqbar, not mentioned in the legitimate edition or, for that matter, in other recognized reference works. Sometime later, *A first Encyclopaedia of Tlön XI: Hlaer to Jangr*, full of related and disturbing knowledge, is left in a bar by a depleted-looking Englishman. His sudden death by brain hemorrhage makes Borges finder of and heir to the volume, which one may suspect of being rough on its readers.

From the abandoned volume, Borges learns of a planet, Tlön, that is idealistic in the sense in which philosophers use the term. Ideas and actions have more power to determine reality than concrete forms do. For example, someone seeking an object can bring it into being through the intention to find it, regardless of its existence elsewhere. This state of affairs is not believed to have occurred naturally; a popular conjecture is that a secret committee long ago conspired to make the planet function according to idealist principles. Whether or not Tlön's basic premise is deliberately programmed—something the reader can never know—once the design is set in motion the consequences unfold without supervision. The study of Tlön's culture shows that the primacy of ideas and processes has profound effects. The most memorable example is the way in which language reflects the altered situation. Where earthly languages employ nouns, one of the two original languages of Tlön, as reconstructed by scholars, has impersonal verbs with affixes carrying the force of adverbs. To describe the moon rising over the river, a speaker would say the equivalent of "Upward, behind the onstreaming it mooned" (English *Ficciones* 23; Spanish *Ficciones* 21; it should be noted that Borges's original Spanish version gives this translation from Tlön language in English). The other great linguistic rootstock has as its dominant feature the stringing together of sequences of adjectives without connecting matter. In the thought of Tlön, space scarcely matters, while time, in which actions and thoughts unfold, is accorded thought and study. But time itself is differently conceptualized; the past can be influenced just as the future can.

Of Borges's many discoveries, the last leaves him overwhelmed. He finds evidence that the outlook of Tlön has begun to contaminate Earth and supplant its traditional habits of mind; the school system has already become a tool in the spread of idealism. Unable to assimilate these discoveries, he writes them into the account of his investigations and withdraws to his hotel room to submerge himself in an intricate work of translation.

"Tlön, Uqbar, Orbis Tertius" clarifies why Borges's stories are sometimes called philosophical tales. The imagining of alternate worlds is a long-standing exercise among philosophers. The priority that concepts and processes enjoy on Tlön is clearly a projection into everyday life of the idealism more usually developed at a much more abstract level. To explain why Tlön is unlike Earth, the narrator alludes to the Irish philosopher generally considered the pioneer thinker of idealism. But the reference, in the form of Hume's comment on Berkeley, cited by the narrator in "Tlön," is not a straightforward discussion of the philosophical truth or falsity of idealism, but rather a tangential observation leading to Borges's story. Hume has noticed that, for all its strengths, Berkeleyan idealism continues to be intuitively unacceptable to the human mind. A subsequent footnote purportedly giving Bertrand Russell's opinion on matters is an even more vivid reminder that Borges, in his invention, has long left behind the terrain of philosophical discussion. Borges's Russell supposedly took the occasion, in the midst of a treatise on the mind, to conjecture that Tlön was newly created and its inhabitants only believed themselves to be remembering a past.

Although "Tlön, Uqbar, Orbis Tertius" takes philosophical ideas and alternate worlds as a point of departure, the interest lies in imagining the consequences a philosophical notion might entail if applied to everyday life, and in speculating on the human cognitive and emotional response to these consequences. In "Tlön" Borges envisions the results of idealism in various areas of human endeavor; for example, the subjectivity produced by the supremacy of ideas over objects reduces all the disciplines to one, the study of the operations of the mind. Of equal concern is the narrator's response to his discovery of the encroachment of Tlön's system on Earth. Obviously disturbed by these revelations, he has nonetheless managed to produce an orderly account of them. The composition of the report appears to have as its purpose to give the narrator himself some reassurance. As he notes, nothing will stop Tlön's idealism once it has begun to supplant Earth's materialism, and consequently he has no more pressing task than to keep his mind occupied with the order-creating task of textual organization.

"La muerte y la brújula" ("Death and the Compass") is a detective story in the same way "Tlön" is a science fiction story; that is, both follow more closely Borges's innovative tendencies than they do the conventions of the popular subgenres they might appear to represent. Besides its kinship to detective fiction, the story is famous for its use of Borges's knowledge of, and fascination with, Jewish mystical tradition. "Death and the Compass" provides an introduction to cabalistic concepts of the hidden divine name and the magical effects to be obtained by evoking it in elliptical form. These notions are set forth with almost pedagogical straightforwardness; at one point, the narrator gives a running summary of the passages in a book on cabalistic lore that the main character is reading. Still, this load of information is fully part of a story of obsessive detection, pursuit, and entrapment.

The detective who is the protagonist is one of many Borges characters who, near the outset of the story, fall prey to some unshakable idea that drives them into a given course of action. Erik Lönnrot is called in to solve the murder of a scholar attending a conference of Talmudic commentators. While his more prosaic colleague follows customary investigative procedures, Lönnrot throws himself into the study of the victim's books on Jewish mysticism. Fixed into a single vision of matters, he states that he has decided, with the investigation barely under way, what type of explanation he wants the case to have: a "rabbinical" one.

As peculiar as Lönnrot's desire for such a solution may seem, subsequent events seem to bear out his insistence that the killer is working with mystical concepts of the name of God. The crime is only the first in a series, with the culprit leaving more and more indications that a cabalistic scheme underlies the violence. Drawing on cabalistic learning, the detectives follow a trail of clues on a complicated itinerary through a fantastic urban landscape, a bizarre and distorted version of Buenos Aires. Pre-Lenten carnival celebrations are under way, and so figures costumed as animals or wearing jester's motley wander through the streets. Rhomboid shapes become a recurring note in the narrator's many observations on the surroundings. The city's small-time crime lords, here treated as an exotic collection of legendary eccentrics, appear in various connections; one of these, Dandy Red Scharlach, seems to have some exceptionally close connection to Lönnrot and his quest. Informative asides and descriptive details, seemingly harboring some hidden meaning, are so numerous and various as to be overwhelming. References abound to aspects of Jewish thought and life that particularly excited Borges's admiration, and such longtime enthusiasms as the philosopher Baruch (Benedictus) Spinoza receive passing allusion.

After a long immersion in his studies, coordinating his newfound expertise on mysticism with the clues the murderer has left, Lönnrot believes he has the case solved. He undertakes a journey to the scene of the next crime. Related with the same confusing abundance of descriptive commentary, the trip takes him through scenes of a city in decay and suburbs where buildings and streets are falling into disrepair. His destination is a country estate that is a monument of neglect, from its rusted gate, through the labyrinth of an overgrown garden, to the house where Dandy Red Scharlach awaits him. Scharlach reveals himself as the adversary who, relying on Lönnrot's propensity for total absorption in one idea, has been manipulating him with cabalistic clues in order to lure him to his death. Lönnrot becomes the last victim in the series. He is among those Borges characters whose fatal weakness is a susceptibility to exclusively narrow and rigid patterns of thought (others are brought down by their desire to hold too much in the mind simultaneously).

The motivation for the final murder is that the detective and the gangster are so disturbingly alike that their identities overlap and, in Scharlach's territorial view of matters, compete for space. For example, the fact that *scharlach* and *rot* are both German words for *red* implies that the characters bearing these names have fewer than two identities between them. Feeling challenged by this encroachment on his selfhood, Scharlach eliminates his perceived rival.

It is a strategy typical of Borges to plant in the mind of a poorly educated or even primitive character the idea that discrete individual identity is a fragile convention. While intellectual protagonists might be expected to brood about their identities, it is more impressive to show a man of action recognizing the ease with which individuality can dissolve. The criminal mentor in "Tom Castro, the Implausible Imposter" seizes upon this principle to perpetrate a swindle, while the gangster Red Scharlach, angered at having to share his identity, defends his turf against a challenger. Further Borges stories reveal an inchoate sense of this same idea in the minds of a variety of rough characters more concerned with survival than with introspection.

"El jardín de senderos que se bifurcan" ("The Garden of Forking Paths") was considered the epitome of Borges's emerging fictional mode when it was first published in *Sur* (1941) and became the title story of his first collection in this genre (since 1944, a subsection of *Ficciones*). It has since receded to a somewhat less outstanding place among the stories.

"The Garden of Forking Paths" is a sophisticated variant of the spy thriller. Its protagonist is classifiable under a number of cultural affiliations. In his diverse life, he has come to owe debts to many individuals and collectivities, and he fails to honor all these obligations of loyalty. Yu Tsun, Chinese by birth, has disregarded the civilization of his homeland despite enjoying privileged access to its high culture. He has developed strong ties to English language and culture, but is a World War I spy for Germany. He is particularly eager to satisfy his superior in Germany and so, he imagines, absolve Asians of the suspicion of cowardice.

The story opens in the disorientingly indirect manner of many Borges stories. A third-person narrator is encountered quoting verbatim, from a standard military history, a dryly informative passage that hardly sounds worth calling to anyone's attention. This anonymous narrator then refers the reader to a further document he claims will help illuminate the historical passage. The subsequently transcribed text, which is said to be missing the first two pages, turns out to be Yu Tsun's account, composed while awaiting execution, of the final episode in his career of espionage.

Yu Tsun finds himself isolated in the English provinces, his prime connection dead. His problem is how to communicate to the Germans the location of a British artillery park, which the Luftwaffe will be eager to bombard. The first part of his chronicle is dominated by Yu's vivid images of his own inadequacy and insubstantiality. He fantasizes his voice trying to call out to his superior in Germany but feebly falling short. A new strategem, though, restores him to strength and action. He murders a prominent sinologist named Albert; the news coverage will send to the German intelligence chief the name that is also that of the town where the artillery park is located.

This spy plot is tangled with a second narrative concerning the reading and appreciation of literature. Yu Tsun, an English teacher and an admirer of Goethe, has turned his back on his own tradition. He has neglected something that constitutes, in a strikingly literal way, his legacy or patrimony. The work of his great-grandfather, Ts'ui Pen, has been languishing for lack of readers competent to comprehend and appreciate it. Yu himself is heard to disparage his ancestor's novel, *The Garden of Forking Paths*. Unwilling to invest thought in his reading— for Borges, a major dereliction—Yu had abandoned the work when he discovered it deviated from standard chronological progression. Albert, before being murdered, offers him a vision of the grace and intricacy of traditional Chinese civilization; his house and its mazelike grounds are a magnificent oasis of this culture in the midst of the English provinces. The sinologist then supplies Yu with the key to organizing the information in Ts'ui Pen's masterwork. Albert's research has revealed that Ts'ui's two great projects, a labyrinth and a narrative, are a single creation, a novel perfectly consistent within its own laws of organization. While labyrinths are usually sinister creations in Borges's work, Albert's Chinese landscape and Ts'ui's novel are two exceptions.

In both cases, Albert is revealing to Yu delights that he has previously failed to appreciate.

This second plot becomes a counterpoint to the tale of espionage. Ts'ui's novel makes sense only when one recognizes its unusual treatment of time. The clue to how to approach the novel is the notable exclusion from its pages of the word *time* and of any discussion of time, thus drawing attention to the term and concept. In the same way, by eliminating Albert from the population, Yu signals to his German boss the most important new development in the war effort. This parallelism is the most evident of a number of correspondences between the two plots. For example, as a spy, Yu has accumulated ill-paid debts of loyalty; as a literary reader, he is guilty of perpetuating the widespread dismissal of his ancestor's contributions.

The visit to Albert's house helps to redress certain negligences in both areas: Yu can now prove his worth to his German commander and render due respect to his great-grandfather's work. But in absolving himself of these long-standing claims of loyalty, Yu commits a fresh, and worse, betrayal. He murders Albert after the sinologist has given him knowledge of great personal and cultural value. Treacherous ingratitude is the dominant feature of the murder; Yu asks Albert to show him Ts'ui's commentary on his novel again, then shoots him in the back as he is retrieving it. Of the many cases of betrayal occurring in Borges's stories, Yu's is one of the most inevitable. The fidelity he owes leads in too many competing directions; he inhabits a labyrinth of loyalties.

Without authoring a novel, Borges developed many projects for works in this genre, leaving descriptions of these plans in his short stories and essays. "The Garden of Forking Paths" contains one of the most appealing. Ts'ui Pen's novel does not discard the possible courses that events might have taken. All potential outcomes of situations are written into the text and can be traced, like forking paths, by a reader who has mastered the system of the work.

"Examen de la obra de Herbert Quain" ("An Examination of the Work of Herbert Quain") presents the career of a writer who pursues with unswerving devotion his unusual principles of fictional construction. The text takes the form of a survey of the recently deceased Quain's contributions. Its author is a man of letters eager that his should be the definitive commemorative essay on Quain. The nerve-grating mode of expression of this affected and self-serving critic gives the story a satirical coloration. In cruel mimicry of the "fine writing" of literary journalists eager to upstage their subjects, Borges has afflicted the narrator with a precious, cloyingly sprightly style. This vain critic cannot keep his envy and rivalry under control; beyond denigrating his colleagues' efforts to memorialize Quain, he persistently finds fault with the work of the very author he claims to be championing.

Herbert Quain is another novelist preoccupied with the representation of time. His most important novel, *April March* (Quain's works appear cited in English in the original), develops a chronological scheme in which the occurrences narrated in the first chapter are then traced backward to divergent possible causes. Three alternative second chapters offer three chains of events that might have led up to the action of the first chapter. Nine third chapters are required to do justice to the variety of precipitating events that might have entailed what is narrated in the three second chapters. Quain's novel stops at this point, though, according to his memorialist, it forms only the third part of a larger project—one may assume, a trilogy that grows ever more multiple and massive as it proceeds toward the opening sequence of events. It is easy to identify the governing concept of Quain's novel as the inverse of the one behind Ts'ui Pen's *The Garden of Forking Paths*.

Quain's other literary inventions, sketchily described, stand out for the feats of concentration and imagination Quain expects from readers and spectators of his work. His detective novel, *The God of the Labyrinth*, reaches a solution only to cast it into doubt. The reader should reread the work, exercising greater skepticism and insight than the detective. The novel reportedly went unread amid the enthusiasm for a rival work of more conventional design; the detail is one of Borges's many sour reflections on the reading public. In Quain's only dramatic work, events of the second act reprise those of the first but give them a mysteriously sordid taint. In this case, the intellectual public favored the work but understood it in Freudian terms—a type of interpretation that revolted Borges, especially as applied to his own work. Although little is overtly stated about Quain's character, the story encourages a degree of empathy with him. He appears to have carried out his eccentric projects in faithful observance of a personal program of literary innovation. His uncompromising purity contrasts with the self-promoting strategies of his memorialist and with the uncaring idleness of the reading and theatergoing publics.

"La biblioteca de Babel" ("The Library of Babel") takes the form of a dramatic monologue or testament. While Borges's stories are often thought of as intricately plotted, a surprising number forgo a sequence of actions and instead present a characters's reflections. The speakers in these stories are tormented individuals struggling to devise some version of their circumstances that will bring them peace of mind. They characteristically are trying to set their thoughts in order while awaiting death, which may be imminent either by execution or, as in "The Library of Babel," through old age.

The narrator is a librarian, following the only occupation in a universe entirely composed of a vast library. This collection is believed so complete and powerful that it holds the entire informational content of the past, present, and future. Yet its resources are nearly unavailable for human use; their unintelligibility to users frustrates communication in a way hinted at in the place name, Babel. After a lifetime dedicated to tending and investigating the library in which he was born, the narrator is eager to believe that there is purpose or meaning in the laboriously maintained collection. His statements constitute a general introduction to the library with special attention to the investigators' search for some system that, if discovered to govern the enterprise, would justify the labors of its staff. He believes himself to have hit upon the solution to this research problem. The closing lines of the story contain the conclusion that represents, for him, a satisfying revelation.

The perspective of the story's readers is unlike that of the librarians, in that the former have no vested interest in the proposition that the library makes sense. The divergence allows for a comically distanced view of the strenuous efforts of the narrator and his fellow librarians to provide a rationale for their operation. At the same time, the story implies that readers are essentially like the librarians of Babel, whatever the area in which they conduct their searches for meaning.

Most of the books in the collection not only cannot be read by local contemporaries, but seem inherently unreadable in any time and place. These works beyond language are exemplified by a book-length run of pages containing nothing but the cluster "M C V" repeated from the first line to the last. Certain books are considered capable of revealing great insights, including the interpretive keys to the other texts. Tantalized by the unreachable wisdom they perceive in these books, a sect of dissident exegetes arises and flourishes for a time. Adepts select promising passages and run them through random permutations and other cryptologic exercises until readable variants occur. This practice is eventually banned for its heretical reliance on chance. Yet offering as it does hope for meaning, it can never be completely suppressed. Other assertions about the significance of the recalcitrant books succeed in winning adherents. The narrator entertains the proposition, which enjoys support in one region of the library, that the books mean nothing and the work of interpretation should cease. Although he does not refute this position entirely, he determinedly maintains that all possible patterns of significance should be investigated.

Not only do the individual books suggest a chaos that can barely be made to appear as design, but the collection itself has only the most tenuous claim to order. Early in the story, the narrator describes the library's layout, giving the impression that this plan allows for systematic distribution of books. His subsequent comments gradually reveal that section librarians do not know what their particular hexagons contain, while no administrator or governing body can supply an overall picture of the location of materials. Again, divergent beliefs arise and compete to explain where and how the design of the system might be encoded. There is a persistent hope that one book may allow the librarians to decode the order of the others, if the volume containing the initial key can be located. It is in the discussion of the library's organization that the narrator believes he has made a contribution. His assertion that the library follows a cyclical pattern, repeating itself once it has exhausted a certain series of possibilities, gives him considerable comfort that his lifework has not been pointless.

There are indications that the librarians are living in a decadent phase of civilization. The most striking of these occurs when the narrator marvels at the precision of the lettering in the books, which, in comparison with his hand lettering, seems to him surely the work of a god. The implication is that the craft of printing has become unknown and that the writing and publication of books have ceased. Other indications of decline and abandonment include the frequent references to the dilapidated condition of the library facilities. From this series of hints, it is possible to argue that the library and its books represent a universe created by a god who has since deserted it. Still, this hypothesis is only a possibility; the story also offers hints that no design ever organized the library.

The Library of Babel is one of Borges's most impressive metaphors for a universe perpetually threatening to overwhelm its inhabitants with too much unusable information. While the librarians may seem ridiculous with their claims and counterclaims and competing sects, the protagonist's determination to extract meaning and pattern cannot be called foolish. The story affirms the need to shape some type of order out of chaotic circumstances. While the narrator describes his discovery rather sketchily, it is clear that to reach it he has had to eliminate some of the available information about the library; not everything he has included in his testament is compatible with the conclusion he eventually advances. Forgetting—the necessity of which is illustrated in several Borges stories—seems to be the mechanism by which the narrator achieves a vision of the universe capable of satisfying his need for order and purpose.

The short stories of Franz Kafka, earlier mentioned as one of Borges's enthusiasms, can easily come to mind when reading "The Library of Babel." The story is constructed as an allegory of all human endeavor and tends to give this striving an absurd and grotesque aspect. The librarian, who has spent his entire life toiling away within the cramped interior of his workplace, sleeping upright in the cabinets provided for this purpose, resembles those Kafka characters whose outlook is formed in narrow, monotonous circumstances. The parallelisms are evident enough that it is not too surprising to find the name Qaphqa given to a sacred latrine in the library.

"La lotería de Babilonia" presents an effort to organize the arbitrariness of human fate (I am using Anthony Kerrigan's *Ficciones* translation, "The Babylon Lottery"; "The Lottery in Babylon" is John M. Fein's translated title in *Labyrinths*). The purpose of the lottery is not to abolish the random factor in life, but to mete it out by means of a systematic and well-regulated mechanism. The central paradox of devising strict rules to preserve the accidental character of events is seconded by many other large and small absurdities. While most Borges stories include comical twists and complications, there is no doubt that "The Babylon Lottery" is especially full of amusing convolutions. The narrator, though, seems unaware that his explanations may strike anyone as funny as he proceeds through a historical account of the lottery, apparently for the benefit of foreigners. A citizen of Babylon, he fully accepts the idea of the lottery and straightforwardly represents its effects on those who see themselves as players in this immense game of chance.

The lottery in Babylon is believed to be under the governance of a secret society known as the Company. Like the committee said to have determined how reality should function on Tlön, this body is so hidden and subtle that its operations are difficult, and at times impossible, to distinguish from naturally occurring events. According to the narrator, who gives the most generally accepted version of matters, the original lottery was simple, but it grew complex when fines began to be assigned along with rewards, making the results stand out more vividly by contrast. Monetary gains and losses were supplemented by good and ill fortunes that would affect the person more directly; a winner might receive a high post, while a loser might suffer imprisonment or become the object of a murderous attack. The definitive evolution occurred after an uprising among those excluded from the lottery. Its status as an elite club was called into question when a slave stole a ticket designating the holder to be burned with an iron. In the ensuing controversy, some argued that the slave should receive his fate as assigned, others that he should take the punishment for theft, which happened to coincide with the fortune he had drawn in the lottery. After this famous case and its repercussions, the lottery was generalized so that all free male Babylonians were automatically participants. The lottery, as it has emerged from this crisis, is entitled to interfere in all aspects of life. Now it is as if the traditional metaphor of the Wheel of Fortune had been made literal.

As ridiculous as the proliferating rules for the lottery become, belief and participation in the lottery have subtly positive aspects. As the narrator proclaims at the outset, "Like all men in Babylon, I have been proconsul; like all, a slave. I have also known omnipotence, opprobrium, imprisonment" (English *Ficciones*, 30; Spanish *Ficciones*, 67). This aspect of the lottery appears to be the one he most values, as he offers it as the first thing to be known about the Babylonian system. The variety of fortunes and misfortunes virtually certain to befall each citizen is the only indication that the lottery indeed exists and functions and also the only reason to admire the phenomenon. In Borges's work, high worth is set on the ability to become someone new, or a number of other people, and to shift from one aspect or facet of experience to another. The Babylonians enjoy such fluidity not only through their diverse range of fates but, more significantly, by the continual awareness that they and their circumstances could become radically other than what they are. The lottery may or may not exist, but the concept has undeniable effects on the consciousness of those who believe themselves participants. The narrator's evident excitement over the lottery and the possibilities it opens is testimony to its efficacy.

"Tema del traidor y del héroe" ("Theme of the Traitor and the Hero") is a brief story with an ingenious plot. The narrator tells, at second hand, of the research a historian friend of his undertook, with results so disturbing they were suppressed. The problem involved is the identification, at a century's remove, of the murderer of an Irish revolutionary leader, popularly celebrated as a martyr to the cause. As the historian sorts through documents concerning the episode, he is troubled by too many, and too perfect, resemblances to the plot of Shakespeare's *Julius Caesar*. He eventually deduces that the revolutionaries had discovered their leader to be an informer and, to avoid demoralizing their supporters, had arranged for him to die in an apparently glorious fashion, using Shakespeare's text as a guide.

In an extra twist, the traitor behaves heroically toward the end of his career. He assigns a colleague to identify the informer who has been ruining the revolutionaries' plans. Presiding at the meeting where the results are announced, he signs his own death sentence, but his name is deleted so that the circumstances of his death do not damage the movement.

Borges's notion of a conspiracy to shape and program reality reappears here. The historian comes to suspect that the revolutionaries left clues to their strategy, but kept them so subtle that the plot would not be uncovered for a considerable length of time. By the time his investigation is complete, he has come to feel part of the entire elaborate machinery set in motion by the inventors of the cover-up. When he sets aside the results of his research to publish a standard heroic biography of the revolutionary leader, he does so with a sense that this course of action also follows from the original conspiracy.

Although "Theme of the Traitor and the Hero" is one of Borges's more popular works, as demonstrated by its frequent inclusion in anthologies, it has not much lent itself to extended critical discussion. The density of narrative information relayed in less than five pages, including two different framing stories, leaves relatively little room for the symbolic elaboration that often draws textual analysts to Borges. The success of a film version (*The Spider's Stratagem*, directed by Bernardo Bertolucci) also supports the notion that this narrative exercises its appeal essentially through its well-composed plot.

"Tres versiones de Judas" ("Three Versions of Judas") features another character who paradoxically stands as a figure of both the traitor and a hero. The starting point for this story is the notion, which has enjoyed currency at various times, that Judas Iscariot should be celebrated for his sacrifice, which helped set in motion the Christian scheme of redemption. Judas's sacrifice is considered exceptionally great, since by betraying Jesus he had to renounce his honor and, in some variants of the idea, condemn his soul to hell.

The complications inherent in this idea are compounded when Borges implants it in the mind of Nils Runeberg. Runeberg is an obscure turn-of-the-century theologian invented by the author to exemplify the type of mentality that can be entirely dominated by an idea. To this fanatical interpreter Borges attributes an apocryphal set of scholarly publications, cited with mock precision, and a history of public rejection by fellow theologians horrified at the deviance of the ideas he expounds. Runeberg's vision goes further and further in exalting the condemnation of one's own soul as the highest sacrifice. Starting by attributing this form of martyrdom to Judas, he later extends it to God, of whom Judas—and not Jesus—is the true transform. The theologian comes to desire such condemnation for himself and hopes to have earned it through his pronouncements.

The idea of significance and wisdom hidden inside language and of the attempt to recover them comes into play in "Three Versions of Judas." The theologian's name immediately brings to mind the ancient runes, which were not so much characters in an alphabet as markers used to encode secret knowledge for transmission among initiates. Runeberg, a modern Swede, does not revert to these pagan practices, but he finds a rough equivalent in the notion that God has a secret name that only the most devoted student of sacred writings could ever identify, and that ought never to be uttered (here Borges is drawing again on Jewish mystical thought). By finding God's name, *Judas*, in plain sight in the Gospels and by attempting to make this finding known through his major treatise, Runeberg hopes to have sinned in the gravest way possible. The offense is not heresy but blasphemy; the latter category of sin, while it has many subtypes, always occurs through utterances and writing and involves the misappropriation of words bearing sacred meanings.

"La secta del Fénix" ("The Cult of the Phoenix") is, at four pages, one of Borges's briefest stories from this period. It is best known for the narrator's refusal to identify the ritual that binds together the worldwide membership of the cult of the Phoenix, although many pieces of information about this ceremony are given in the course of the text. The narrator does not himself belong, but over the years he has come to know a great many adepts of the Phoenix and discover the one activity that confers unity on the group, whose members are otherwise indistinguishable from the general population.

The shreds of information given about the nature of the ritual lead the imagination in more than one direction. A number of them suggest that sex is the matter not discussed. For example, the rite is performed in secret, and allusions to it, especially inadvertent ones, can make initiates either smile or look uncomfortable; young adepts cannot expect their mothers to explain the matter, but must seek guidance from some person of outcast social status. Yet other information about the ceremony is ridiculously incompatible with this supposition. Most incongruously, the ritual is performed with a piece of cork and some wax and gum arabic; this set of specifications effectively rules out most of the hypotheses readers might form about the nature of the action.

Along with the tantalizingly equivocal and oblique characterization of the central ritual, "The Cult of the Phoenix" is distinguished by the presentation of a favored Borges idea, the conspiracy so subtle and unobtrusive as to shade off into the natural course of events. Late in the story, it is revealed that modern followers of the Phoenix no longer perform its rite, preferring to allow the meaning formerly localized in the action to pervade their relations with divine forces. Some now believe that the cult is evolving into something entirely internalized, comparable to an instinct. These considerations are reminiscent of the committee that may or may not have choreographed the idealist reality of Tlön, the company that may or may not govern the Babylon lottery, and the gods who may or may not have made the library in Babel. In each case, there are two distinct ways of understanding the issue. If one believes the speakers, the original conspiracy was and is real, but its workings have grown so sophisticated as to be almost undetectable by outward signs. Seen in this way, the stories present an outlook similar to the theological notion that the universe was created and set in motion by divine fiat, but currently operates without any form of superhuman intervention. A second interpretation is that the narrator, along with many others, has fallen prey to the lure of conspiracy theories, and is attributing hidden, preconceived designs to naturally, arbitrarily occurring events. This reading would make the stories into tales of mass delusion, and so into commentaries on the strength of the human desire for complete explanations of all matters. The evidence for or against a conspiracy remains equivocal, and the narrators themselves note, in the thought of their contemporaries, divergent beliefs concerning this problem.

The narrator of "Funes el memorioso" ("Funes the Memorious") is another fictional representation of Borges. He has been a personal witness to the case of a Uruguayan country boy who lost the ability to forget and died under the burden of his own indiscriminately accumulated, unsynthesized memories. The narrator is one of several persons who had contact with this oddly cursed individual and who have agreed to set down their impressions in writing. The rationale he gives for this undertaking is to document a phenomenon of scientific interest, but he obviously feels personally involved with the questions raised by Funes's abnormality and appears to be composing his account in great measure to gain a satisfactory perspective on the entire matter. When the narrator first encounters Funes, the young man has not yet been overpowered by memories he cannot organize. There are signs, though, that Funes stores in his mind elements that other people release. Borges's country cousin shows Funes off as a local curiosity for his infallible recall of proper names and his ability to tell the time without looking at the sun. Later Borges, on another rural vacation, hears that Funes has been paralyzed in a riding accident and has had his longtime eccentricities curiously exacerbated. He receives a note from Funes requesting to borrow Pliny's *Natural History* in Latin and a dictionary to that language. The idea of mastering a Latin text with nothing but a lexical guide seems absurd, but when Borges visits Funes, he finds him reciting from the work. Funes comments on the passage in question, dealing with prodigies of memory; he considers the feats of recall described to be unremarkable. Borges then becomes the privileged confidant to Funes's account, which lasts all night, of losing the ability to expunge data from the mind.

Funes's relation, which Borges partly summarizes and partly quotes verbatim, occupies about half the story and constitutes its real reason for being. It is one of the best examples of the author's ability to recreate the point of view of an individual living under radically abnormal conditions. The following extract, from James E. Irby's translation in *Labyrinths*, is from this much-cited portion of the story:

> We, at a glance, can perceive three glasses on a table; Funes, all the leaves and tendrils and fruit that make up a grape vine. He knew by heart the forms of the southern clouds at dawn on the 30th of April, 1882, and could compare them in his memory with the mottled streaks on a book in Spanish binding he had only seen once and with the outlines of the foam raised by an oar in the Río Negro the night before the Quebracho uprising. These memories were not simple ones; each visual image was linked to muscular sensations, thermal sensations, etc. He could reconstruct all his dreams, all his half-dreams. Two or three times he had reconstructed a whole day; he never hesitated, but each reconstruction had required a whole

day. He told me: "I alone have more memories than all mankind
has probably had since the world has been the world." (63–64;
Spanish *Ficciones*, 123)

Not only can Funes not forget, but he cannot subordinate certain
remembered items to others. He lacks an inner hierarchy that would
keep significant matters more vividly present in his thoughts while
relegating trivial ones to the background. Consequently, he cannot
perform even such basic functions as shifting the focus of his attention
or forming a generalization from specific examples.

The story gives particularly detailed information about Funes's
symptoms, which are in each case charged with meaning. The common
local belief is that Funes was paralyzed by the impact he suffered on
being thrown from a horse; however, Borges encourages the understanding that Funes is unable to move under the accretions of memories
he can neither dismiss nor subsume under general categories. Funes's
death is attributed to pulmonary congestion. Although such an end is
realistically likely for an immobilized individual with a paralyzed dia-
phragm, it is more in tune with Borges's symbolic approach to see the
boy as blocked with remembered elements that cannot be absorbed
into his system or expelled. One of Funes's physical problems, severe
insomnia, is directly attributed to his incapacity to forget. His confi-
dences to the narrator include a technique for clearing the mind to
induce sleep. While arcane and bizarre bits of advice at times appear
in Borges stories (for instance, how to find the center of a labyrinth),
the remedy for sleeplessness is full of common sense. In their disarming
plainness, these recommendations especially bring home the necessary
association between the purging and editing of one's thoughts and the
ability to function.

The main issue examined in "Funes the Memorious" is, beyond
doubt, the need to organize knowledge in the mind by means of judicious omission and the selective concentration of attention. Another
strong concern is the idea of the catastrophic miracle. In a number of
Borges works, characters have managed to attain powers beyond the
usual range of humankind, but they have become grotesque and disturbing superbeings. This secondary theme is evident in the contrast
between Funes's way of describing his condition and Borges's manner
of speaking of the topic. Funes, boasting of his powers, tells Borges
that his world is immeasurably rich and that paralysis has been a small
price to pay for the plenitude of experience he now enjoys. Borges, in

contrast, perceives Funes as a rare pathological specimen, an extreme case that can illuminate the mysteries of consciousness. Rather than mourn Funes's death, Borges regrets that this phenomenon was not more thoroughly evaluated by experts on the malfunctioning brain while the boy was alive.

"Las ruinas circulares" ("The Circular Ruins") is particularly likely to appear in anthologies and by all accounts is one of Borges's most popular works. Its wide appeal may owe much to the treatment of magical rites of creation, which Borges here describes in detail and in an unusually respectful tone. Borges can be acidly satirical in his characterizations of mystics and practitioners of magic; for example, the possessor of the oracular Aleph, discussed in Part 2 of this volume, is one of the most cruelly ridiculed buffoons in all of this author's works. Yet the magician who brings a man into being in "The Circular Ruins" is a serious creative artist within his odd area of endeavor. His lengthy ritual exertions are in no way absurd or deluded, and his final disillusionment, which does nothing to invalidate his magical achievements, occurs with a measure of dignified pathos.

The story's epigraph, given in English in the original, is Lewis Carroll's "And if he left off dreaming about you," an allusion to the concept that human beings are figures in the dream of some superior entity. The line from Carroll gives the initial clue to the revelation that ends "The Circular Ruins." Between the epigraph and the last paragraph, though, this disturbing suggestion is set aside in favor of a careful account of the magician's long struggle to summon a full-grown man out of dreams.

The narration of the creator's labors is exceptionally successful in its evocation of a world ripe with miraculous possibilities. The opening sentence contains the single most extensively discussed lexical choice in Borges's work: the night in which the magician arrives at his ritual site is described by an adjective that, in ordinary speech, could never be used for this purpose: unanimous (English *Ficciones*, 52; Spanish *Ficciones*, 59). The conviction that magic may occur on this chosen island is strengthened by a number of particular items of information. Most notably, the wounds with which the magician comes to its shores are healed when he awakens from his first sleep there. Augmenting the suggestion of an exceptional world is the elevated, solemn tone in which the story is told. While Borges's narrators are often full of mischief, providing misleading hints or coyly claiming to be missing vital information, the speaker in this story gives every sign of making his best effort to relate events he considers significant.

The work of dreaming a man into existence confronts the magician with certain problems that repeatedly form the core of Borges stories. He first dreams a classroom full of students, looking for a likely candidate to be brought into individualized being. The practice leads him to the discovery that those who cannot stand out among his general impressions of the class, and so cannot become the focus of his thoughts, have no potential for breaking through into reality. The best candidates to achieve reality distinguish themselves by being an attention-demanding irritant to the dreamer's mental life. What he learns is the much-repeated Borges notion that the mind must be able to select the most salient portion of a totality in order to register it in any meaningful fashion. In di Giovanni's translation: "After nine or ten months he realized, feeling bitter over it, that nothing could be expected from those pupils who passively accepted his teachings but that he might, however, hold hopes for those who from time to time hazarded reasonable doubts about what he taught. The former, although they deserved love and affection, could never be real; the latter, in their dim way, were already real" (*The Aleph and Other Stories*, 57; *El Aleph*, 61).

Before his creation can succeed, the magician must learn other difficult lessons. After his first new beings fail to prosper, he is driven to consult, again in dreams, a statue that reveals itself as the god of fire. The advice this god offers makes the mental creation of a human being sound tellingly similar to the raising of a naturally conceived child as well as to the presentation of artistic work. The new being cannot thrive until its maker takes the step of sending it away to another ritual site located on the same island. As well as the parent's obligation to loosen its hold on a maturing child, this requirement parallels the creator's need to give autonomy to his or her work when it goes out among audiences who read it in ways beyond authorial control.

As he develops a sense of concern over his absent creation—now plainly referred to as his son—the magician is eager to protect this being from discovering his status as someone else's dream. The magician has learned that fire could discern and manifest the new being's lack of autonomy, and would like to spare him what he imagines to be a shameful and degrading discovery. In the final twist, it is the creator who experiences this glimpse of his own insubstantiality and dependence. With fire engulfing the site of his ceremonies, "he walked into the leaping pennants of flame. They did not bite into his flesh, but caressed him and flooded him without heat or burning. In relief, in humiliation, in terror, he understood that he, too, was an appearance, that someone else was dreaming him" (*The Aleph and Other Stories*, 61–62; *Ficciones*, 66).

"The Circular Ruins" is an indirect reflection of Borges's celebrated concern with Jewish mystical tradition. The legend of the Golem, mentioned earlier as one of his adolescent discoveries, appears in this story, but considerably transformed. The creator here uses an eclectic form of magic. His way of proceeding can hardly be called rabbinical; uninhibited by the prohibition against idolatry, he consults the statue of the fire god (though only after he has reached the depths of frustration). A worker of cabalistic spells would rely on sacred writings, tapping powers of creation latent in their very characters; in most versions, the Golem is brought to life by applying Hebrew letters, constituting an elliptical form of the sacred name, to its inert body. This protagonist makes his own dreams his text and at times seems to be practicing a magic suitable for preliterate peoples. Despite these obviously divergent notes, the story does reestablish contact with Borges's cabalistic currents of thought. The most significant of these clues occurs when the magician, revealing a considerable store of learning despite his current isolation from the literate world, considers a reported effort among members of a Gnostic sect to create a new Adam. Gnosticism is Christianity's main point of intersection with cabala, and the story of the man-made Adam looks distinctly like a version of the Golem legend. More specifically, it resembles Borges's reworking of the Golem tradition in his poem "El Gólem," included in the 1969 collection *El otro, el mismo* (The other, the same one).

The mystical and magical elements in Jewish tradition make a less disguised appearance in "El milagro secreto" ("The Secret Miracle"). The plot of this story is unusually easy to summarize: a moment before his execution by firing squad, a man is granted one year's reprieve to finish a dramatic work. A year of composition unfolds entirely within his mind and no other person present detects any alteration in the flow of time. Perhaps because of its simple and elegant plot, centered on one exceptional event, "The Secret Miracle" became the first Borges story to appear in English in a publication aimed at a fairly general audience. Harriet de Onís translated it to include in the 1956 bilingual anthology she edited for Pocket Books, *Spanish Tales and Stories* (this version appears reprinted in *Labyrinths*).

Prague at the moment of its occupation by Nazi troops is the setting for "The Secret Miracle." The historical catastrophe coincides with a critical moment in the career of the protagonist, Jaromir Hladík. Hladík is tormented by a cluster of preoccupations that, as the narrator points out, are common to writers. He would like his writing to justify his existence, but cannot identify any work with such powers among the books he has produced so far (his anxiety on this point provides the opportunity for another detailed supply of spurious bibliographic information). Now he has—partly written but mostly still in his mind— a dramatic work that he hopes will reward and infuse with meaning his entire struggle for creation. The story gives a schematic characterization of the projected work, which never reveals whether it holds the special potential its author sees in it. At least the play can be seen as a worthy attempt, for it follows certain aesthetic principles that Borges himself has long promoted. For example, Hladík has chosen to compose his drama in verse so as to remind audiences that art is, in fact, artful.

With Prague occupied, Hladík reasonably fears he will never complete his project. He is likely to be among the first of the victims of the Nazis, not simply as an individual of Jewish ancestry but as a propagator of Jewish culture. His most distinctive specialty, which would be as repugnant to the Nazis as it would be appealing to Borges, is to uncover the traces of Jewish thought hidden in artifacts of Western civilization without overt Jewish content. A treatise on the Jewish sources of Jacob Boehme, the Protestant mystic, is his prime achievement in this subtle and controversial field of research. He has also done work in cabalistic interpretation, translating the *Sefir Yetzereh*, one of the two great canonical works in this area of endeavor that combines study and commentary with mystical devotion and magic.

All these elements come together when Hladík is, indeed, condemned and faces the possibility of dying without carrying out the work that will give his life worth. After praying for a year's extension of his existence, he experiences a dream charged with significance. In it, he enters the great Clementine Library. Its attendants have been unable to locate, in the many texts under their care, the one letter that could open direct human-divine contact. Hladík, his hand evidently guided, soon touches the letter and hears a voice from all around him granting his prayer. These and other details make the point that not only is the miracle revealed through powers cabalistically come into the world through the word, but it is Hladík's thorough study of Jewish sources, mystical and rationalistic both, that allows him to understand and participate in this extraordinary event.

While the wondrous favor Hladík receives necessarily dominates the story, the question of writing and its worth is also strongly present. "The Secret Miracle" is one of several Borges stories that take place directly after a writer completes his lifework, offering occasion for judgment. Here Hladík's situation permits him to survey his own career from what he is convinced must be its end point, although later he receives an extension. More typical is an arrangement in which a commentator, usually somehow involved with the author, offers a posthumous overview. While such retrospectives can present the fictitious author's work in an entirely favorable light—such a case will be seen in "Deutsches Requiem" from *The Aleph*—in most instances, great uncertainty remains as to the enduring value of a writer's accomplishments. Of particular concern to Borges are those authors whose claim to significance rests on an endeavor that must be either a distinctive contribution to literature or else nothing more than the symptom of an unshakable delusion. Among these writers who may have been serious innovators or mere eccentrics, the most famous and extensively analyzed example is the title character of "Pierre Menard, Author of *Don Quixote*," among the most critically esteemed Borges stories.

The narrator, who has undertaken a posthumous commentary on Menard's work, is an obsequious member of the French literary scene. Borges is unsparingly satirical in providing this self-important man of letters with irritating affectations, particularly a fondness for showy and attention-getting lexical options (Borges has often spoken of his efforts to cure himself of a desire to impress by his choice of words). The narrator's motives for memorializing Menard are less than pure. With his stylistic pirouettes, he betrays a desire to upstage the author he is promoting, and he is eager to establish himself as the one person most capable of explaining the misunderstood genius of Menard. For all his insufferable ways, though, the narrator actually has grasped the subtleties of Menard's project and gives a good account of it. The same paradoxical relation between a literary work and its commentators figures in a number of Borges's texts. The character presenting an author's achievement seems unworthy of being the one to explicate it. For example, in the extreme case of "Deutsches Requiem," a Nazi war criminal characterizes the work of a humanistic Jewish poet, while other discussants are unable to disguise their envy or resentment of the author in question. Still, through the impenetrably contradictory workings of art, communication and understanding have evidently occurred; just as good literature is not necessarily produced by good people, a defective human being can be an outstandingly perceptive reader of literature.

Although Menard eventually emerges as an admirably earnest figure, the first part of his story casts the value of his lifework into doubt. The narrator begins with a methodical listing of Menard's published oeuvre, characterizing each item briefly. The resulting image of Menard is that of an author enmeshed in a snobbish coterie made up partly of writers and partly of wealthy patrons that the former flatter and amuse. Some of Menard's publications aim to please, in a servile way, his powerful friends; others show isolated bursts of eccentric originality, but without any coherent vision. In a complicated joke, Borges makes Menard's career parallel at points (i.e., in his choice of publication venues) that of Paul Valéry, the poet whose often wild-sounding pronouncements have proved most stimulating to literary theorists. Yet Menard also represents aspects of literary life that Valéry satirized, and has undertaken projects meant to denigrate Valéry and his achievements.

The account of insubstantial and even tainted accomplishments comes to an abrupt end when the narrator exhausts the published portion of Menard's work and announces with a flourish: "Now I will pass over to that other part, which is subterranean, interminably heroic, and unequalled, and which is also—oh, the possibilities inherent in the man!—inconclusive. This work, possibly the most significant of our time, consists of the ninth and thirty-eighth chapters of Part One of *Don Quixote* and a fragment of the twenty-second chapter. I realize that such an affirmation seems absurd; but the justification of this absurdity is the primary object of this note" (English *Ficciones*, 44–45; Spanish *Ficciones*, 48–49).

The remainder of the story is taken up with explaining how these statements can possibly be the case and with giving Menard's beliefs about his project of writing *Don Quixote* in the twentieth century. The narrator cites at length a letter he received from Menard. The extracts show the modern author of *Don Quixote* to be no simple monomaniac, but rather someone who has given careful thought to general theoretical issues in literature (his outlook is similar to Borges's own expressed views) as well as to his own peculiar undertaking. To the reader's relief, Menard's letter is free of the self-promotion and posturing that mar his commentator's writing and make his praise of Menard suspect.

The letter not only presents Menard in a favorable light but makes the point that his project is an almost purely conceptual enterprise, belonging as much to literary theory as to artistic creation. It is the only useful evidence by which the reader can judge Menard as a writer of actual prose, even though other citations from his work appear in the text. These latter quotations provide no information about Menard for an obvious reason: they are identical, word for word, with the equivalent passages of *Don Quixote* (the narrator helpfully cites the original for comparative purposes). The exact repetition of Cervantes's words paralyzes the usual critical faculties, and Menard's work can be evaluated only at a very high level of abstraction.

The fundamental idea behind Menard's *Don Quixote* is that it would be a more difficult, and therefore more valuable, task for a twentieth-century Frenchman to compose this work than for its original author to bring it into being for the first time. As well as the obvious differences in linguistic capabilities and cultural frames of reference between the two authors, there are some complicating factors that involve questions of literary theory. Menard is determined to write *Don Quixote* as a twentieth-century man and not to attempt to recapture the perspective Cervantes once had. The reason for this rule is not just to make his work more difficult, although Menard definitely believes that art should be undertaken in the face of near impossibility. The gap of centuries between Cervantes and Menard has produced changes in *Don Quixote* itself. The work's significance has been enriched by many generations of readers who have added their individual and collective understanding of the text to the totality now thought of as *Don Quixote*. In this sense, the novel as it exists now is a more meaningful version.

Menard's ideas about the reading of works from earlier eras are essentially those of the major tendencies in twentieth-century literary studies—the various formalist and structuralist movements and, most particularly, New Criticism. These movements discourage readers from attempting to re-create the way a work was originally read, not only because such an exercise will always fail, but also because literary works grow in meaning through successive readings and interpretations. With Menard's extreme application of these precepts, Borges brings out the absurd possibilities inherent in modern literary criticism. Yet he is not ridiculing Menard in order to discourage other critics from holding the same basic ideas. The paradoxes that Menard engages in during the course of his experiment can be comical, but they are contradictions that Borges himself recognizes and would like to see examined.

Menard's way of treating *Don Quixote* also brings into question the veneration accorded a classic or a masterpiece. At the same time as *Don Quixote* has been supplemented by the attention paid it by perceptive readers, it has been obscured by the tendency to enshrine it as a classic; none of Cervantes's contemporary readers were constrained, as are today's, by the conviction that they would be deficient if they failed to find enduring significance all through the novel. Menard believes he can overcome this inhibition because, as a reader from outside the Spanish-language literary tradition, he does not perceive *Don Quixote* as an immovable foundation stone of his culture, and so can take a more fluid and imaginatively freer view of it.

Many other ideas receive memorably original treatment in this story, especially in those portions of it supposedly transcribed from Menard's letter. In living through his own experiences in such a way as to arrive at the writing of *Don Quixote*, Menard believes himself to be ushering in a new age of mental flexibility. His ideal is that any given individual should be able to hold, as if it were that person's own, any idea, and then to release it and move on to other thoughts. Though Menard's commentator is personally obnoxious, he adds several worthwhile reflections on his subject's chief preoccupations. Among these is the observation that while Cervantes had recourse to realism—that is, based his art on real-world material—Menard juxtaposed one literary text with another and so operated more purely in the world of art and ideas, scarcely having to set foot among the untransformed realities of everyday life. These and other notions sound like those Borges often expressed, which suggests that Menard, however shaky the value of his major work, still had a vision meriting respect.

Although Menard's literary thought involves serious issues, its realization in the new *Don Quixote* can still be the occasion for mischievous jokes. The commentator makes himself ridiculous by launching into a contrastive analysis of the styles in which the two *Don Quixotes* are written. Menard's is deliberately archaic and hence somewhat affected, while Cervantes's is much plainer and more straightforward. The commentator eagerly cites the distinguishing features of the two styles, apparently having driven from his awareness the fact that the exact same words in precisely the same sequence are involved in both cases. Comic, too, is the elaborate secrecy with which Menard conducts his experiment. Even the commentator, who would like to be the ultimate expert on Menard, cannot say how Menard took years to produce small portions of *Don Quixote*; he can report only that the author filled page after page, used a number of curious symbols, and was in the habit of lighting public fires to dispose of his drafts. In his zeal to be Menard's intellectual heir, the narrator urges a further application of the principle behind the new *Don Quixote*: readers should approach certain works as if these had been authored not by their actual creators but by other writers with a different set of cultural associations; he closes his essay with a suggested set of incongruous pairings of authors and works.

"La forma de la espada" ("The Shape of the Sword") is a brief and relatively uncomplicated example of Borges's stories of traitors and those they betray. Again, betrayal appears as a peculiarly intimate act, as well as a traumatic one; it leaves its mark on the perpetrator (in this case, literally as well as metaphorically) and creates an inescapable bond to the victim.

The narrator is a city man who on his occasional visits to the country hears about, and sometimes witnesses, the dramas of local life. He becomes fascinated by an Irish immigrant famous for a crescent-shaped scar across his face, his periodic retreats into drunkenness, and his severe dedication to running his lands. The Irishman takes the narrator into his confidence and tells the story, which is transcribed verbatim, of his life in the country's anti-British guerrilla forces. John Vincent Moon, a revolutionary with an undisguisable cowardly streak, is at the center of this narrative. The scar-faced man reports feeling personal shame at Moon's behavior, as if he were implicated as well. Finally he caught Moon informing on colleagues; he heard his own name mentioned to the British. He then pursued Moon and managed to cut his face deeply before being taken prisoner. After recounting this narrative, he confesses that he is John Vincent Moon.

The story provides a paradoxical context for discussion of one of Borges's favorite concepts: the boundaries of individual identity are so fragile that anyone may be contaminated with another's traits. The special twist in this case is that these reflections are spoken by Moon. He recalls feeling his fellow revolutionary's cowardice as if it were his own failing; it actually is. This circumstance does not disqualify Moon's statement that one individual can become another or, indeed, all human beings. Still, Moon's version of this principle is too simple to account for his case. If the transfer of selves were unequivocal, he could just as easily lose his identity as a traitor, but clearly it has remained to haunt him. The story as a whole makes the point that one person communicates to another elements of identity, but the transfer gives mixed and uncertain results. The self that results from such comingling is an unstable, plural entity, exemplified by the narration of the sorely divided Irishman, who speaks in two competing identities.

"El fin" ("The End") adds one more episode to a lengthy narrative poem well known to the Argentine public. *Martín Fierro*, which José Hernández published in two parts in 1872 and 1879, centers on the dissolution of the gaucho culture that once flourished on the Argentine plains. Martín Fierro is an emblem of the rebellion (which, however, he eventually abandons) against the government's campaign to convert the pampas to farmlands, eliminating the open-range system vital to the nomadic ways of the gauchos. During his wanderings, he kills a black man in a knife fight.

The episode Borges adds is simple: seven years later, the dead man's brother seeks out Martín Fierro and challenges him to a knife fight; this time Fierro dies. The matter grows more complex in the actual elaboration of the story. The encounter between Fierro and his victim's brother is seen, in great measure, from the point of view of a man who keeps a frontier tavern. The proprietor does not speak for himself, and indeed is incapable of doing so. But the narrator tells of events in the order they came to this observer's attention and describes this character's thoughts and reactions, as well as giving further commentary.

Recabarren, the tavern owner, is one of several Borges protagonists who, like the Englishman who dies after acquiring a volume of *A first Encyclopaedia of Tlön*, seem unable to withstand the impact of revelatory events or texts. When the revenge-seeking black man takes up a post near the tavern and begins a series of actions designed to attract Martín Fierro, Recabarren dimly understands that a complex ritual is under way and that he cannot make sense of it in any usual fashion. Rather than adapt to the shift, Recabarren suffers a stroke and registers the further unfolding of events while lying half-paralyzed.

The most cited passage from this story is the account of the knife duel on a stretch of plain drenched in moonlight. In his description, the narrator emphasizes the vague, contourless monotony that the entire scene has assumed. It is explicitly pointed out that, in this inchoate landscape, no possible site for the duel is really different from any other. These indifferentiating notes suggest the importance the fight will have beyond its obvious purpose of revenge. As the victorious survivor walks away from this ritual scene, the narrator first identifies him as being no one, then discovers that he has taken on the essential identity of the man he just killed. The dissolution and transfer of selves is the real struggle behind the knife combat; it is what overwhelmed Recabarren when he sensed its imminence.

"El sur" ("The South") is among the Borges stories most likely to be classified as fantastic. Its climactic episode may represent a fantasy, a dream, a hallucination, or the actions of an already-dead protagonist magically allowed to live out one last adventure. To anchor this sequence of improbable events, the story employs a mode of narration that is unusually straightforward and, particularly in the first half, consistent with the narrative conventions of realism. In many stories of *Ficciones*, the narrator is called Borges but diverges from his real-world model, creating peculiar ambiguities and giving the narrative data an equivocal status. Here the protagonist has many traits known to be those of the author, but bears a distinct identity as Juan Dahlmann and is treated strictly as a fictional character. The task of telling the story falls not to him but to a third-person speaker who has none of the eccentric or mischievous habits common among Borges's narrators.

The first part of "The South" is an account of an episode of blood poisoning suffered by the protagonist, a library worker in Buenos Aires. This evocation of the experience of serious illness has struck readers and critics as exceptionally vivid and true. Its most significant aspect, for the unfolding tale, is the protagonist's sense of humiliation and powerlessness. He is given false reassurances, moved about, shaven, bound, and subjected to unexplained procedures.

This section comes to an end when Dahlmann sets out on a journey that will allow him to become again an autonomous adult and a man. While supposedly he has been released from a clinic to rest at his country place, small oddities suggest that some less ordinary matter is at hand. Though barely convalescent, he is sent out alone to make his way through the city and out to the house he maintains to the south. Further incongruities accumulate as Dahlmann is put off the train in an unfamiliar town and becomes the object of provocative derision from local toughs. When a storekeeper inexplicably turns out to know Dahlmann's name, it is evident that matters are operating by some unexpected new set of rules.

The story ends with Dahlmann stepping outside for a knife fight that, although not narrated, is strongly hinted to result in his death. Dahlmann, amid these quickly unfolding events, manages to grasp that he has received a second chance to die, this time with a measure of style and dignity. In his mind, the area far south of the city, with its rough ways and surviving traces of gaucho culture, has delivered him from his reductive, civilized death. Dueling with knives, a spectacular element of gaucho culture that has persisted in the face of urbanization, helps Dahlmann replenish his sense of being Argentine—a feeling that has been attenuated by living a life indistinguishable from that of a contemporary European city dweller.

While not offering grounds for the extensive critical commentary elicited by such playful, intellectual stories as "Tlön, Uqbar, Orbis Tertius" and "Pierre Menard, Author of *Don Quixote*," "The South" is an important Borges text. Critics have often referred to it when discussing the relation between Borges's work and fantastic literature. It has exercised strong popular appeal for its memorable plot, the immediacy of its descriptive passages, and an engrossing lyricism uninterrupted by the satirical and whimsical notes that Borges often uses to create a reflective distance.

The Aleph

The title story of *The Aleph* would certainly be on any list of Borges's five top stories. It summarizes his work in a number of ways and is a good source of insights into his fiction in general. It is memorable in part for the figure of the Aleph, capable of presenting the cosmos so that it can be seen simultaneously, though not in any ordered or synthesized form. In offering a plot concerning the Aleph, the story implicitly encourages readers to maintain a suspicious attitude toward the cheap appeal of unmediated revelation and to value, instead, the truths conveyed through artful, selective representation. The story's other compelling feature is the attitude and behavior of the narrator, who, unlike the hermetic protagonists of many of Borges's stories, has easily recognizable emotions on open display.

The narrator, who bears the name Borges, is suffering from persistent grief and from the realization that the memory of his great love, Beatriz Viterbo, is slipping away. His desire to retain a hold on the long-dead Beatriz locks him into a disagreeable pseudofriendship with her cousin Carlos Argentino Daneri, who eventually proves the lead to the Aleph of the title. Daneri fills Borges with revulsion and jealousy, but continues to exercise an attraction as a means to the recovery of Beatriz. Borges in turn supplies the captive audience Daneri requires for his recitations of and commentary on an interminable poem he is composing. Daneri, who is presented by the irritable and rivalrous Borges as a figure of self-delusion, believes he can bring all facets of Earth together through this poem.

While quotations from Daneri's poem confirm Borges's low opinion of his actual writing, there are clues that Daneri's motivation is not so different from an impulse that works upon his derisive listener. Borges, too, would like a vision of totality, though not of the world but solely of his Beatriz. When he describes himself examining photographs of her, he is clearly tantalized by images that render only one aspect at a time. As later events prove, though, such an incomplete, never-definitive representation is the one that can most successfully lay hold of his imagination. Like a cryptic, elliptical text, the photographs present an artistic form of truth about the many-sided Beatriz.

The suspicion that the two characters share a common urge for totality is confirmed when Daneri invites Borges to see, under a stairway in the cellar, the Aleph that supplies his poetic material. Borges suspects that the poet is mad, but allows himself to be positioned on the floor with his head at a certain slant. "Then," as he admits, "I saw the Aleph" (*The Aleph and Other Stories*, 26; *El Aleph*, 163). Moreover, he describes it and tells what knowledge he obtains from it. Such explicit treatment of a revelation is an unusual feature in Borges's fiction, where the narrative often breaks off immediately before the vision or else describes its sensory effects but not the information revealed. In this case, readers find out what the oracle divulged, but the contents turn out to be worthless. The total vision of Beatriz, far from fulfilling Borges, leaves him feeling assaulted and defrauded. Instead of the perfection he had sought, he encounters aspects of Beatriz that disgust him. Most significantly, the image of Beatriz is so full of information that it is essentially false, even if everything it contains is true. A uniform, indiscriminate, unnuanced spew of data cannot do justice to the complexity of the human being, whose nature is to be now one thing and now another. It is particularly inadequate in the case of Beatriz, who had charmed Borges with her changeability, ambiguity, and unpredictability, qualities lost in the overload of information that the Aleph automatically discharges when perceived. In his enamored quest to reassemble Beatriz, Borges has not stopped to consider that to construct an ideal, or any other type of meaningful image, requires the suppression of some information about the real-life model (the necessity of oblivion is a favored Borges theme). It is imperative to forget, discard, or avoid acquiring data, procedures incompatible with the pursuit of a complete revelation. Borges embarrassedly retreats from the mechanical and lifeless truth of the Aleph, judging it false.

The treatment of the Aleph in this story directs attention away from this phenomenon and toward the two characters who manage to find it. For example, the word *Aleph*, after appearing in the title, is absent from the first part of the story and remains undefined until well into the text. It reappears and is explained only after a great deal has been established about Borges and Daneri. The attention given to their reasons for craving the Aleph suggests that the magic sphere is brought into being by force of desire and enjoys no existence unless sought. Borges again is commenting on the determination of human beings to master some absolute form of knowledge. Daneri wants to own, in a literal way, access to total information; he is eager to retain property rights to the cellar containing the Aleph. Borges is more sophisticated than the poet, but, his judgment weakened by his massive grief, he also falls into the mental patterns that create the Aleph.

The story presents three principal examples of the diverse forms Aleph-seeking can take: Daneri's poem "Earth," Borges's campaign to preserve all information concerning Beatriz, and the sphere in the underground chamber. Other similar endeavors are mentioned in passing, suggesting that human beings, in their frustration with the necessarily tentative and incomplete nature of knowledge, are frequently engaged in the quest of the Aleph.

Among the elements of this story that have most interested critics, the ironic reprise of Dante is one of the most pursued. Daneri's name looks like an elliptical form of Dante Alighieri's, and his poetic project superficially seems ambitious in the same way as the *Divine Comedy*. Beatriz is quickly identified with Dante's ideal woman Beatrice. These and other parallelisms bring out the fallacy that makes Daneri and Borges fools of the Aleph. While Dante grasped that an ideal woman should remain largely unknown, Borges tries to maintain an image of perfection while seeking to assemble all knowledge of his Beatriz. Daneri is even slower to grasp that to be absolutely all-encompassing, or even completely representative, is both an impossible and a useless enterprise. He determinedly loads more and more heterogeneous elements into his monstrous poem, in defiance of the commonsense principle that art requires selectivity and the repetition of significant uniformities.

The contrast between the great poet and the story's characters makes the point that, while all human beings may harbor a desire to have something absolute and total, not all are equally apt to succumb mindlessly to this craving. In "The Aleph," Borges and Daneri make their mistakes through unawareness of basic principles or ground rules for the construction of knowledge. Borges, more intelligent than Daneri, grasps the nature of his mistake and pronounces the Alephic vision false by reason of its senseless amassing of truths. Dante is a wiser figure because he understands from the start that, even in a sweepingly grand project, inclusivity is not worth attempting. Among the implications of this story is the warning that one should be conscious of Alephs and the human susceptibility to their allure.

"The Zahir," while it is an independent story, is also a counterpart to or mirror image of "The Aleph." These two reciprocal stories became anomalously separated as Borges's texts began to reach an English-language readership. "The Zahir" was the first Borges story to be presented to a significant audience in English; Dudley Fitts's translation appeared in *Partisan Review* in February 1950 and was collected in the 1962 *Labyrinths*. "The Aleph" was curiously bypassed by translators into English until Norman Thomas di Giovanni selected it for the 1970 *The Aleph and Other Short Stories*, which, however, does not contain "The Zahir."

The title of "The Zahir," like that of "The Aleph," refers to a magical object that Borges has adapted, for its symbolic possibilities, from folk sources (in this case the traditions of the Arab world are cited). Even if the Aleph and the Zahir do not originally occur in the same cultural system, in Borges's world they stand as counterpoised extreme possibilities, an A and a Z of thought. In Borges's treatment, the Aleph overwhelms its viewers with too many items to consider; the Zahir stands for monomania, single-mindedness, and fixed forms. Physical objects can be the Zahir; the "Borges" who is protagonist and narrator of this story receives the Zahir as a coin that contaminates him with an idée fixe. More important, though, the Zahir can sum up a pattern of thought riveted on one thing. Just as Beatriz Viterbo is encapsulated in the Aleph, the dead woman Borges remembers in "The Zahir," Teodolina Villar, becomes the Zahir.

Although the Aleph and Zahir represent symmetrical figures, they are unequal in complexity and interest. The Aleph, streaming forth uncontrolled information, excites the mind, even if it cannot satisfy it. Gazing into the Aleph leaves Borges suffering from the effects of overstimulation. The Zahir, in contrast, is distinguished by its predictability, and its effect is numbing. Rather than overwhelm with too much new data, it enters the mind to erase or suppress ideas and associations that were hitherto present, making room for thoughts of its own and not very interesting self.

The event that precipitates the encounter with the Zahir is Borges's attendance at Teodolina's wake. Unlike the compelled, haunted pilgrimages to Beatriz's home described in "The Aleph," this visit is the conventional discharge of a social obligation. Teodolina has lost the claim she once had on Borges; he is repelled and bored by her unvarying pursuit of, as he puts it, perfection in preference to beauty. In all areas of life, she seeks only to observe protocol and follow fashion. Borges, thinking back over her life, recalls some comically grotesque examples of her single-mindedness, such as her concern that a Nazi-occupied Paris might be unable to transmit new fashion designs. While the errant, capricious Beatriz can provoke enduring love and rancor, the monotonous Teodolina leaves Borges little about which he might care.

Borges departs the wake in need of fresh air; he walks through the urban night landscape. His description attributes to this environment a fluidity oppressively absent from Teodolina's life. The welcome openness of the street scene continues into a tavern Borges then visits. He observes customers playing cards; games of chance and strategy, which involve risk and conjecture, contrast with the certainty and closure Teodolina demanded. Yet the vision of free play is brief, since Borges receives as change the Zahir. He cannot dismiss this object from his mind. Subsequently Borges learns that he is not the only one with his thoughts involuntarily trained on one object; a plague of monotonous preoccupation with the Zahir is ravaging the area and threatening to engulf humankind. Perhaps because both the woman who emblematizes the Zahir and the monomania the phenomenon provokes are unexciting (Borges compares Zahir-fixation to anesthesia), this story is notably less cited than its counterpart. The urges that drive seekers to the Aleph are dynamic forces and, fittingly, the characters react to one another and to the false promise of the Aleph with love, hatred, and longing; in contrast, those consumed with thoughts of the Zahir lose their lively qualities.

Although the stories "The Aleph" and "The Zahir" belong to Borges's second volume of short stories, the two central concepts offer keys to the tales in both the 1944 and the 1949 collections. Looking back through the earlier series of stories as well as surveying the later ones, readers could recognize, as clues to interpretation, many variants of the Aleph and the Zahir.

This insight, which in its general outlines has probably been reached independently by any number of Borges readers, was formulated and applied with exceptional clarity in Wheelock's *The Mythmaker*. Wheelock sees Borges's stories as centered on the concept of the hypostat, one aspect or feature of a reality that is momentarily elevated above all others and comes in for special attention. Hypostatization is necessary to the mind's workings, but it is difficult to maintain a flexible balance between the perception of a totality and the singling out of particular components. The Aleph and the Zahir represent complementary failures of this process; a person caught up in the Aleph is unable to focus mentally, while affliction with the Zahir prevents the victim from releasing a hypostat once it has served its purpose. These two disorders can easily merge, so that certain situations and phenomena in Borges's work are capable of triggering both fixation and a misguided striving for all-inclusivity.

"Abencaján el Bojarí, muerto en su laberinto," like a number of Borges stories, brings together two characters who are reciprocals or mirror images of each other. ("Ibn Hakkan al-Bokarí, Dead in His Labyrinth," is the title of Norman Thomas di Giovanni's translation, which uses this restyled form of the character's name throughout. It should be noted, though, that in English-language discussion the name is often given as in the original Spanish.) Of the two, one is the traitor and the other the betrayed. A recurring theme in Borges's fiction is the relation that arises from treachery; it appears as an especially intimate tie. The complementarity of their roles binds, and at times blends, perpetrator and victim; the transfer of attributes from one to the other, or the exchange of their identities, can result.

"Ibn Hakkan" offers two explanations of a murder that took place in a great red labyrinth, an English seaside house now fallen into ruin. The version favored by the local population makes the chieftain Ibn Hakkan the victim of a vengeful ghost from whom he had vainly sought shelter in his rambling mansion. The ghost is that of his vizir Zaid, known for his cowardice, who had helped his master abscond across the desert with a treasure. The greedy chieftain had stabbed his sleeping accomplice, but before dying Zaid swore the vengeance that was eventually accomplished in the mazelike house. Ibn Hakkan's words and behavior support this account; he had expressed apprehension that the ghost might find him in England and, shortly before the discovery of the body, had reported his house actually under attack by Zaid's spirit.

An imaginative and sensitive observer, Unwin, works out another version of events, starting from the contradiction between Zaid's established cowardice and the idea that he would allow himself to be taken in his sleep. Unwin surmises that Zaid abandoned Ibn Hakkan in the naturally occurring labyrinth of the desert. The English house was built not by Ibn Hakkan but by Zaid, assuming his victim's identity. Its purpose was not to elude the vengeful, betrayed partner but to attract him. The ploy was successful in bringing Ibn Hakkan into a terrain where Zaid could enjoy every advantage in killing him. The body in the house, with its face battered into unrecognizability, was that of the real Ibn Hakkan, and the person the locals knew by that name had fled with whatever remained of the treasure. Unwin's explanation provides a more satisfying account of the known phenomena than the locally popular ghost story does, and the process by which he reached his conclusions inspires respect for his intellect and understanding of humankind. Still, the story offers no definitive confirmation of Unwin's solution, such as the confession by the guilty party that provides the closure for many detective tales. The lack of proofs suggests that, like many assertions made in the course of Borges's stories, the propositions Unwin advances win out by their artistic truth.

This tale offers a number of aesthetically pleasing and symbolically functional symmetries. It pairs a yellow, natural labyrinth, the desert, with a red one built by human beings, the English house, and sets parallel scenes of betrayal in the two mazes. The name of one of its linked protagonists, rendered Abencaján in the original Spanish version, begins the alphabet, while that of the other ends it. The stories of *The Aleph* encourage readers to perceive the Aleph and Zahir in many guises; they here seem represented by the paradoxically twinned characters. Unwin decodes the generally accepted version of events by identifying significant correspondences and reciprocities and running them through a series of transformations. The version Zaid would have people believe thus turns out to conceal a second story that is like a distorted reverse image of the first. As Unwin puts it to an upholder of the locally popular explanation: "The facts were true, or could be thought of as true, but the way you told them they were obviously lies" (*The Aleph and Other Stories*, 122; *El Aleph*, 130). First the roles of betrayed and traitor must be reassigned between the chieftain and his vizir. Zaid unwittingly signals the inversion of identities when, posing as Ibn Hakkan, he claims to have left the dead Zaid faceless. The obliteration of the face would then have been pointless; instead, it is a strategy Zaid is saving for his anticipated encounter with the real Ibn Hakkan. The purpose of building the great red house is the destructive counterpart of the protective motive its owner gives. (This last reversal exploits an inherent paradox of the labyrinth. In Greek myth, it is a means both of protection and of entrapment; Daedalus built one to protect the Minotaur and to ensnare human sacrifices to this monster.)

The short story often served Borges as a means to reevaluate in public his longtime preferences in literature. "Ibn Hakkan" is a sign that his fondness for Chesterton is undiminished. Among the tributes to Chesteron embedded in this story are the provincial English setting and the local vicar to whom the false Ibn Hakkan tells his distorted version of events. Unwin, like Chesterton's detective Father Brown, comes upon the solution to the crime through "knowledge of the human heart," starting with the realization that a true coward would never sleep in the company of his partner in crime and proceeding on the assumption that a liar's story will betray elements of the hidden truth.

"Los dos reyes y los dos laberintos" ("The Two Kings and Their Two Labyrinths") is a brief tale (less than a page and a half long) reflecting on "Ibn Hakkan." Appearing directly afterward, it reprises and inverts the plot of the longer story. It, too, features an initial act of cruelty and a fresh outbreak of conflict when the aggrieved victim reencounters the man who wronged him. In this case, the initial offense takes place in a constructed maze and the second meeting involves the already-existing labyrinth of the desert, a recapitulation in reverse order of "Ibn Hakkan." In addition, the seeker of revenge, who in "Ibn Hakkan" seems only to find a more definitive defeat, in "The Two Kings" more than repays the man who earlier trapped and confused him.

"The Two Kings" is also distinguished by the coloration Borges gives to the narrator's outlook. This storyteller is a pious follower of Islam. The viewpoint of staunch believers fascinated the skeptical Borges; in literature, he took advantage of this type of thought as a source of paradoxes. Here, the teller of the tale states his disapproval of the magnificently puzzling construction in which the first king imprisons the second. To his mind, the building of such an artifice is a usurpation of functions that should be exclusively divine. The first king does not kill his entrapped victim, while the second one ravages his enemy's lands, captures him, and leaves him to die of thirst and hunger. Yet the narrator is less severe with the king who abandons his rival in the desert, a labyrinth properly created by the working of divine powers.

"La casa de Asterión" ("The House of Asterion") is distinguished principally by the unusual choice of narrator and the careful way in which this speaker's point of view is represented. The text presents itself as a monologue by the Minotaur, a type of deposition he has formulated and now recites (he is illiterate) to explain himself to anyone concerned. In an era in which Borges's stories are famous, readers may well know before beginning the story that it reelaborates the myth of the Minotaur. For the original readers, the identity of the voice speaking was an enigma to be guessed from the extraordinary statements the speaker makes about his experience of the world.

In the well-known myth, the Minotaur, with its bull head and human body, was the unfortunate product of the mating of a sacred bull with a king's wife. Considered a sign of shame as well as a monstrosity, this creature was confined in the labyrinth built for this purpose by Daedalus. Periodically, young people were sent into the labyrinth as sacrifices to placate the Minotaur. The last of these, Theseus, mastered the system of the maze by tracing his passage through it with a thread, killed the monster, and escaped.

The details of the classical myth scarcely interest Borges, and indeed he freely alters specifics in order to convey the dimensions to which he gives significance. Most interesting is the reconstruction of how the mind of the Minotaur would work. Nearly the entire story is the Minotaur's explanation of matters, revealing a vision of the world formed by someone who has rarely ventured forth from his labyrinth. The Minotaur is also at a disadvantage in conceptualizing, because he has no fellow beings against whom he might measure himself and must interact, on anomalous terms, with people. With this extreme instance, Borges is able to give an exaggerated version of the solipsism that affects those living under more usual limitations.

The Minotaur's account of himself is a complex one, alternately calculating and unguarded. His monologue reveals a good deal more than the effects of a cloistered existence. Intelligence, and with it a capacity for dissimulation and rationalization, complicates the monster's outlook and expression.

Although he has no way of seeing his situation as it would appear to the world outside, the Minotaur has begun to grasp that he is not finding the rewards life should seemingly be able to offer. Repeatedly he wards off an intolerable awareness of aspects of his situation by giving to events the most favorable interpretation possible. Nonetheless, the suspicion that he may be profoundly defective in both his person and his situation threatens to break through to an overt level. For instance, the Minotaur claims that his failure to master reading arises from the grand sweep of his intellect, impervious to such minutiae as letters of the alphabet. Then he admits that illiteracy has been a burden, leaving him with too little to occupy his mind. When the townspeople flee from him in terror and revulsion, he attributes to them all a common set of disturbing facial deformities. He boasts of being unique, but admits to fantasizing about the arrival of a second Minotaur to befriend him.

As the Minotaur nears the end of his statement, there is a pathetic weakening of his efforts to suppress awareness of his miserable state. He finally confesses that his principal hope is for the fulfillment of the prophecy, which he has overheard, of his destruction at the hands of Theseus.

This tormented admission ends the Minotaur's speech, but the story contains an addendum. The postscript narrates an exchange between Theseus and Ariadne, who has helped defeat the Minotaur. Theseus is shaken by the monster's scant interest in defending himself. Certainly the Minotaur's acceptance of death is no surprise by now. The epilogue seems to serve the purpose not of presenting information but of pulling the reader back outside the Minotaur's consciousness and providing a reminder of how greatly his account differs from outsiders' views of him. Ending the story back among normal human beings also suggests that the distortions found in the Minotaur's thought are like those less spectacular ones that shape everyday reality.

"Deutsches Requiem" is another such dramatic monologue emerging from a consciousness struggling to make sense of events and circumstances. In this case, the speaker is a Nazi convicted of war crimes; like Yu and the minotaur, he is giving an account of himself while waiting to be put to death. The story has drawn attention because it contains, although not as its most salient subject matter, fairly evident judgments regarding social and cultural matters. Borges's stories may at times appear so relativistic as to raise concern that no values are endorsed over any others. "Deutsches Requiem," in contrast, unmistakably favors humane civilization over nazism.

Still, its major emphasis is not on social realities; it is a story of concepts warring within the mind. In this case, the protagonist-speaker has difficulty in maintaining a strictly Nazi outlook. The incomplete mastery of a mode of conceptualization gives the narrator an interest and appeal he would not otherwise have. As Aizenberg notes, zur Linde is, among other things, a representative of the Jewish tradition of intellectual culture; he is, despite his efforts to expunge this side of himself, "a German, a man of the West, and hence a 'Jew'" (Aizenberg, 130). Wheelock has pointed out that Borges gives zur Linde many of his own biographical characteristics. Athough his goal is perverse, zur Linde's mental struggle is one manifestation of a type of intellectual effort that, if rightly applied, Borges finds admirable (Wheelock, 162–63).

Otto Dietrich zur Linde confesses to the crimes with which he is charged, but admits no guilt. His monologue is an effort to explain how this can be the case and how he can regard Germany's defeat with satisfaction; in addition, he is still engaged in the effort to clear his mind of any thoughts unworthy of a steely warrior. He argues that strict causality governs the universe. Therefore, it is futile—at one point he says blasphemous—to object to the workings of its inalterable tendencies. This insight should entail the elimination of charity and compassion.

Zur Linde's rationalistic presentation begins to break down and reveal a mind in rebellion against its own officially held tenets. In reviewing his career as a concentration camp officer, he cannot suppress his sense of empathy toward a Jewish poet confined in his facility, even though zur Linde has killed the man in an effort to rid himself of the identification. With his flexible, freely ranging mind and capacity for love and pity, the poet troubles zur Linde as an unwanted double of certain aspects of himself. Zur Linde hints that he drove the poet to suicide by implanting in him a monomania devised for this purpose, clearly a contamination of the victim with something originating in his tormentor. As in many Borges stories, the guilty party and the injured one are bonded in a way that makes the transfer of features between them seem inevitable.

While the story is abundantly paradoxical, its judgment on the specific matter of the Nazis and their victims is not relativistic. The partial identification of the Nazi and the poet does not transfer any of zur Linde's guilt to his victim or attenuate his own responsibility. The Nazi movement is associated not only with genocide and suppression of liberties but with an attempt to destroy the elements that give Western culture its value. One of zur Linde's involuntarily expressed insights is that the Nazis, though apparently driven by a desire for conquest and victory, inwardly knew that their program was deleterious to the world and sought its defeat. Further reducing the possibility of an amoral reading is the characterization of the poet David Jerusalem and his work. Borges had a gift for ridiculing literary people; some of the writers who appear in his stories are eccentrics driven by an unshakable vision, while others are hacks and obsequious climbers (Herbert Quain and Pierre Menard on the one hand, and the critics who present them on the other, epitomize the two types). Jerusalem, though, has nothing risible about him.

In a passage outstanding for its presentation of a divided mind, zur Linde includes in his testimony a general introduction to David Jerusalem's poetry that will explain its exceptional power. In his characterization of the work, zur Linde reveals himself to be as alert and understanding a reader as the poet could hope for. Zur Linde has identified the moving force in Jerusalem's work as an ability to bring now one perception, now another, vividly into focus, letting the rest of the world drop off into mere background. By turning the reader's attention so intensely on a single thing or idea in all its particularity, Jerusalem's poetry fosters in readers the ability to feel tenderness and compassion.

Although zur Linde is well aware of Jerusalem's excellence, he continues to believe in the extermination of the values and tendencies the poet's work encourages. It is through his acute understanding of his victim's poetry that he is able to destroy its maker. Jerusalem has the gift of riveting awareness on a single thing and exalting its importance, but also possesses the fluidity required to move from one thought to the next. Zur Linde succeeds in fixing Jerusalem's mind on one topic (undisclosed in the story) in such a way that the poet cannot disengage his consciousness from its unceasing consideration, until his own extraordinarily intense focus drives him insane.

"Deutsches Requiem" makes evident Borges's habit of showing philosophical ideas as fascinating and beautiful, even when no defense can be made of their truth or, as in this case, their application to the conduct of human affairs. Zur Linde is monstrous, but his choice of purely philosophical concepts is irreproachable. Schopenhauer, perhaps the single philosopher who most excited Borges's imagination, turns out to be a favorite of zur Linde's as well, and both the author and his character are attracted to the same passages in this thinker's work. Yet Borges cannot possibly endorse zur Linde's use of Schopenhauer's concept of a universal Will to prove that even atrocious crimes need entail no remorse.

Zur Linde should be included with the various individuals and societies that, in Borges's fiction, are observed infusing principles of idealism into their everyday lives. The Nazi does not want to think like David Jerusalem, who celebrates concrete particulars; he would like to keep his awareness continually at a high level of abstraction and ignore, especially, the specific features that make human beings touching and appealing. The concept of the superbeing enters into the story's mix of ideas; as elsewhere in Borges, those who surpass human limits prove to be monstrous.

In "Biografía de Isidoro Tadeo Cruz (1829–1874)" ("The Life of Isidoro Tadeo Cruz [1829–1874]"), Borges develops further a character from *Martín Fierro*, the narrative poem to which he had already added an episode ("The End," from *Ficciones*). In José Hernández's original poem, Sergeant Cruz, sent to arrest Fierro, suddenly joins him as a fellow renegade. His decision to go over to the rebellious gaucho's side, cryptically related in Hernández's account, is the center of Borges's addendum.

The teller of Cruz's life story, unlike many Borges narrators, never reveals the sources of his information. He at times affects the expository habits of a historian, particularly in his fondness for exact dates. Still, he is clearly not relying solely on documentation, since his knowledge extends even to the night of Cruz's conception and the unspoken feelings of his rough, taciturn subject. Although he has access to Cruz's motivations and can even articulate his inchoate insights for him, the narrator confesses to odd gaps in his coverage of the sergeant's life. The use of a curiously defective variant of the omniscient narrator heightens the oddity of finding a fresh supply of information about a literary character, who presumably has no existence outside the work in which he appears.

A review of Cruz's past thoughts and actions reveals that, although representing a pro-urban government, he has always shared Martín Fierro's profound aversion to modern city life. The events of his life parallel those of Martín Fierro's biography at a number of points. Both have lived on the run, have been conscripted, and have been responsible for stabbing deaths, though not in the same sequence in the two lives. Finally the narrator states plainly what he has been leading up to: when he comes face to face with the celebrated rebel, what Cruz sees is himself. While many Borges characters arrive at the realization that identity cannot be confined to a single discrete individual, the nature of the revelation varies greatly from story to story. The entire intricate machinery of "Death and the Compass" is set in motion by one man's need to eliminate another who, he has discovered, shares portions of his identity. Cruz, far from conceiving a murderous rivalry toward his double, embraces him, and is instantly transformed into his great companion and ally.

Among the most popular and frequently anthologized of Borges stories, and one of the relatively few to be filmed, is "Emma Zunz." While its plot is ingenious, it consists of a line of events relatively uncluttered by the enormously detailed related subnarratives that complicate many of the stories in *Ficciones* and *The Aleph*. The remoteness and distance that characterize many Borges stories are not part of "Emma Zunz"; the heroine's emotions are strong and unmistakable, and the narrator gives them a prominent place in the account. "Emma Zunz" is also a satisfying tale of revenge: a seemingly passive, downtrodden young woman, after taking cruel blows in life, rallies her forces and through determination and strategy defeats an unscrupulous, powerful adversary.

Emma's sudden burst of vengeful energy is unleashed by news of her father's suicide. The father had suffered imprisonment and disgrace over the disappearance of funds from the factory where he kept the books. The real thief, he had told Emma, was the manager, who escaped suspicion to become a co-owner of the plant. The plan Emma now constructs will allow her to kill the real embezzler, leave a stain on his honor, and escape punishment. She schedules a meeting with the owner, hinting that she wants to turn informer against strike organizers in the plant. Before the appointment, she finds a sailor to take her virginity. She then meets with the factory owner and murders him. Her allegation that he has raped her is compatible with her physical and emotional condition at the time. The narrator, who has been relatively slow to comment on events, ends the story by offering his interpretation: the account Emma gave the police, even though many elements were altered, prevailed because it was true in its essence.

This sequence of actions plays out in an ambience charged with treachery, guile, and suspicion. The event that takes place previous to the story and motivates it is a betrayal, and more such behavior is required to right the wrong. Borges, here as in many stories, reveals a fascination with the expected bonds of loyalty among members of a community and with the violation of those bonds. The initial offense is exacerbated by the traitor's selection of a victim from within his own group (the story draws attention to the Jewish identity of the principals). Emma's plan for vengeance requires her to pose as an informer willing to betray her fellow workers to the owner of the plant. The grim sexual encounter between Emma and the sailor involves little actual deceit, but indicates a breakdown of human community. The two have no common language and seek separate goals. Surveying possible sexual partners, Emma has deliberately selected one who will not draw from her an empathetic response. This tale of revenge culminates in yet another episode of betrayal and deceit. The reader has been led to applaud this last treachery as a corrective to the one that set events in motion.

Even when Borges's work is comparatively straightforward, as in "Emma Zunz," it is still characterized by uncertainties and ambiguities. The narrator knows a great deal about Emma's thoughts and reactions, but he seems unable to supply more easily verified data. For example, the letter telling Emma of her father's death is from someone who may be named Fein or Fain; the sailor who has sex with her may be Swedish, or he may be Finnish. Access to Emma's thoughts is sometimes total, but at other moments the narrator can only conjecture about what is in her mind, prefacing his speculations with "It is my belief that" (*Labyrinths*, 135; *El Aleph*, 62). As elsewhere in Borges, markers of doubt, such as *perhaps* and its equivalents, appear with frequency. These vacillations serve as continual reminders of the impossibility of achieving and holding a stable vision of the world.

"Historia del guerrero y de la cautiva" ("Story of the Warrior and the Captive") is a title that accurately reflects the paradox central to the text. It suggests interaction between the warrior and the captive, but because it is the story of both, the two never meet. The warrior is a Lombard barbarian in the period following the collapse of the Roman Empire; he deserts the tribal armies and becomes a loyal defender of Ravenna, still an outpost of Roman-style culture. The captive is a nineteenth-century Englishwoman taken by South American Indians and absorbed into their tribe. Whether they are nonetheless part of a single story is the question the narrator is eager to raise.

The narrator is another Borges figure, typically concerned less with new information than with how he acquires it and how his mind processes and absorbs it. His material on the barbarian warrior comes to him first, through a brief summary in Benedetto Croce's *La poesia*. It affects Borges so strongly that he imagines in detail the experience that converted the warrior Droctulft from nomadic tribal ways to urban civilization. The anecdote triggers an association with some half-lost recollection. After pursuing several false leads through his memory, Borges recovers the captive's tale, told him by his grandmother, who met the woman in question.

Following the narration of both anecdotes, including his imaginative additions to Droctulft's story, Borges further explores the reasons that his mind would link the two so strongly. The explanation he rejects as too superficial is that the stories are antagonistic. It is true that Droctulft repudiates tribal life and stakes his faith in cosmopolitanism, struggling to master the sophisticated turns of Latin, while the captive switches her loyalty to the tribe and, by the time Borges's grandmother meets her, has nearly abandoned English for an unwritten local language. Still, Borges's closing reflections encourage a longer view of the two cases as a single story in which some inexplicable force impels a person from one community to another.

Several features make "The Story of the Warrior and the Captive" representative of Borges's work. Reciprocal characters who are mirror images of one another and the sharing of identity between two or more individuals are recurring elements in Borges's stories. So is the narrator's curiosity about loyalty to groups and communities, always a troubling and contradictory phenomenon in these tales. A further Borges hallmark is the narrator's scrutiny of his own mind when excited by new data, and his expectation that such introspection, rather than the verification of facts, is likely to bring into being significant truths.

"El inmortal" ("The Immortal") is the lead story in The *Aleph*, though it is not altogether representative of the volume. It is unusual in its length, some twenty pages, and in its leisurely development. Most of the text is a travelogue, a translation of a translation whose original cannot be located; characteristically, there is reason to doubt its authenticity, although the insights it presents are valid ones. An opening note explains that a minor princess found the text tucked into an edition of Alexander Pope's translation of the *Iliad*. The bookseller who supplied the edition, like the Englishman who leaves behind volume 11 of *A first Encyclopaedia of Tlön*, is dead by the time the narrator acquires the text in question. Each of these offstage characters is reported to have been looking drained and worn before he passed along the text and died. The implication seems to be that the original owner of the manuscript was debilitated by the revelations he glimpsed in its pages.

The traveler is a wealthy Roman who had been a tribune, led military campaigns, and grown worldly from his travels through the eastern Mediterranean, but, still dissatisfied with his existence, undertook to become immortal. He has set down a chronicle of his journey to, and life beside, the fabled City of the Immortals. The memoir is notable for its curiously artificial manner and seems to represent a composite of styles and conventions. The introductory passage draws attention to its unnatural qualities with the unsatisfactory explanation that it is a literal translation from the English.

The idea that the achievement of superhuman traits may entail monstrosity is one that appears in a number of Borges texts. In this case, the narrator comes to the City of the Immortals, but is slow to recognize it. As he later learns, the immortals tore down their beautiful city and rebuilt it in an arbitrary and horribly disturbing form. They then deserted it altogether. The deliberately pointless complications of the uninhabited city, which the Roman describes with terror and disgust, are the first indication that immortality is a tainted gift.

The immortals have allowed themselves to deteriorate as if regressing to the prehistory of humankind. The first of them the narrator meets is Homer, but for some time the former is unable to recognize the latter even as a human being. Naked, cave-dwelling, and unkempt, Homer is mute until a burst of rain restores his speech. From the Roman's point of view, and surely the reader's, the epic poet is in a decadent state. Homer, though, with the indifference of the immortals, is unconcerned that he has nearly forgotten his own epic work and his knowledge of ancient Greek. He simply observes that it has been some time since he composed the *Odyssey*.

The other immortals, who live naked in caves near the city they have spoiled, also evidence a monotonous flattening of their emotions and spirit. Without the possibility of death, they have lost all compassion. Since misfortunes invariably prove survivable, there is no urgency to relieve suffering. The members of the city perceive themselves as already being what they will be; they have no sense of themselves as evolving and becoming. The Roman, who had eagerly drunk from the river of immortality when he first arrived, now comes to see that stagnation and numbness are consequences of knowing oneself and others unable to die. The aimlessness, apathy, and torpor all around him suggest that the expectation of death is a necessary stimulus to the development of distinctively human characteristics.

Immortality comes to be odious to the Roman and Homer, who has become his guide and the confidant for his disillusioned reflections. The two set out for a river that can give them back the capacity for death. After centuries of searching, the narrator, at least, obtains a drink of these restorative waters. When he scratches his hand and it bleeds, he is satisfied that he has escaped his terrible venture into deathlessness.

Rereading the story of his immortality, the Roman begins to experience uneasiness. He suspects that its strangeness is the result of a joint authorship with Homer, and shows examples of a fluctuation between Greek and Roman outlook and expression. Since the two did not collaborate in any usual sense, evidence of co-authorship indicates the fusion of their identities. An addendum by another commentator seeks to bring in the bookseller as another author and another dimension of the same collective self. Rather than reaching some resolution, the question of authorship becomes more and more complicated as traces of material by yet other authors seem to appear. The implication is that the attribution of a text to a single author is a deluded, if widespread, practice. The problem is not simply the impossibility of disguising one's literary influences. The maintenance of unique selfhood, always a precarious achievement in Borges's stories, cannot withstand the acid test of textual composition. The act of writing, by forcing writers to draw on the collectively owned repertory of knowledge and skills, leaves them susceptible to the unmistakable interference of alternative selves.

In making the case against immortality, the story focuses less on actual death or invulnerability to death than on the awareness of these conditions. The Roman remarks, early in his chronicle, that all animals except man are immortal by virtue of their ignorance of their own inevitable death. The comment prefigures the regression of the immortals toward the state of beasts. The possibility of death is inextricable from other human possibilities, such as those for change and progress. Wheelock (129) has extended these notions by connecting them to an analogy that recurs in *Ficciones* and *The Aleph*. He argues that in "The Immortal," as in many Borges stories, human beings are seen as ideas held in a vast, divine mind. Following this supposition, individuals who cannot die are like unquestionable dogmas. Mortals, in contrast, are like the changing inventory of concepts held in a mind capable of perceiving matters in various ways.

"Los teólogos" ("The Theologians") centers on another pair of rivals who become interdependently fused. After years of vying to be foremost in theology, one causes the other's condemnation for heresy, though it is an equivocal point whether any real harm was intended. He then witnesses the public burning, the only time he sees his competitor, and lives out his remaining years as an incomplete being, aimlessly moving from place to place.

A good deal of this text is taken up with the discussion of heretical sects of the Middle Ages, particularly the monotonous and histrionic movements (names found, rather than invented, by Borges). Neither of the paired protagonists actually promulgates these heretical outlooks, but their work requires them to discuss the concepts involved. The two heresies represent, at different moments, extreme ways of conceiving of time; in the histrionic vision, time proceeds forward, never repeating itself, while for the monotones, it is circular and redundant. The difference between these sets of beliefs is shown as fascinating to think about, but in a sense trivial. While the histriones are the more complex and interesting heretics, the story's characterization of the two sects encourages a relativistic view of the entire dispute over time and a satirical vision of all those involved in it. In Borges's stories, convinced believers can be exotically bizarre, brilliant, or personally engaging, but they do not appear as worthy exemplars of thought. The most admirable thinkers are always those who can hold different ideas in their minds and shift in and out of conceptual perspectives.

"La otra muerte" ("The Other Death") is among the Borges stories that can most justifiably be called fantastic, as the plot turns on a violation of the evident operating laws of the universe. The narrator is a fictionalized version of Borges, with his habit of investigating odd circumstances of regional history. He obtains confusing results when he makes inquiries about an Argentine, Pedro Damián, who fought in the Uruguayan revolution and participated in the 1904 Battle of Masoller. Damián's commanding officer tells him that the man proved a coward in that combat. On another occasion, the officer has no recollection of Damián, though a wartime comrade who is present remembers him dying a hero's death at Masoller. This latter reminiscence is especially surprising, since Borges knows that Damián died very recently, in 1946. Finally, Damián's commanding officer contacts Borges to state that he now also remembers that Damián died heroically in the great battle.

The rest of the story tells of Borges's efforts to make these conflicting testimonies fit a pattern. He decides that Damián succeeded, through repentance over his cowardice at Masoller, in rewriting the memory of his performance there. He earns a second chance by living out his remaining years in an unspectacular but valiant combat with the harsh back lands of Entre Ríos province. The image of Masoller is first transformed in Damián's own mind; as he is dying, a fever dream transports him back to the battle and allows him to correct his actions. His desire to remake the past is so strong that his heroic version of

Masoller begins to seep backward in time, first erasing recollections and then supplanting them with more favorable ones.

In studying the two conflicting historical realities, Borges cannot rely on such direct methods as obtaining eyewitness testimony. His approach is oblique, accidental, and baroque: he happens across relevant items in the course of reading literary and theological works, which he cites with suspect zeal. These remote sources are aesthetically superior to the rawer and more immediate ones, and they allow Borges to reach a solution.

Still, his account of the matter does not satisfy him for long. He is particularly suspicious of the fact that his best clue came from the theologian Pier Damiani, whose name is all too close to that of Pedro Damián. Borges distrusts the habits of mind he has acquired as a writer of imaginative literature. The story ends with Borges casting doubt on the very answers he has long struggled to formulate.

Although the rewriting of Damián's war record occurs through supernatural intervention, it closely resembles a more pedestrian phenomenon. His retrospective transformation is, in a sense, only an exaggeration of the process by which heroes are mythified. Witnesses' descriptions of Damián's glorious death in battle are indistinguishable from standard accounts of the last moments of any much-celebrated combatant. Here is the hint that any hero might be a transformed manifestation of what was once a coward.

"La espera" ("The Waiting") is known for the mysterious presentation of the ineluctable Villari. The protagonist is an anxious man who tries to flee Villari by taking a room in a boardinghouse in a strange part of the city. Yet it is clear that Villari will inexorably find him out no matter where he goes. From early in the story, there are strong indications that this character is not eluding another person, even if at the most literal level Villari is a rival gangster. To fit all the clues in the story, what the protagonist fears must be some collective entity, not a particular individual or individuals. The pursuer must also be something profoundly inseparable from the fugitive, although he is futilely struggling to break away from it and establish himself independently.

The idea that the protagonist is thoroughly contaminated by and implicated with his pursuer is confirmed when the pursued character is asked his name. He can produce no other answer but Villari, and, in fact, no other name is ever given for the lead character. This incident suggests that *Villari* carries the magic charge of a tribal name and refers to a family or ethnic group, with its powerful ability to exercise inescapable claims. The incident of the name gives new meaning to a remark the narrator had earlier made; the man was pleased that fewer Italians now lived in the neighborhood because he "preferred not to mingle with people of his kind" (*Labyrinths*, 165; *El Aleph*, 137).

Furthering the notion of running away from home is the foreignness the protagonist displays in his new setting, as when he pays out a coin from another country. Many other details strengthen the idea of an unshakable affiliation. For example, the man makes friends with an old dog and speaks to it not only in Italian but in some regional dialect barely remembered from his childhood—a language entirely of the home domain.

The fugitive's encounter with Villari takes places many times in dreams, always according to an identical scenario. The confrontation in dreams and the one that occurs in waking reality, in conjunction, offer clues to the enigma of Villari. In dreams, Villari is always accompanied by two men, but when he appears to the waking protagonist, he has only one man with him. The implication is that the missing third man is the nameless hero, who has temporarily succeeded in fleeing the place he should occupy in the collectivity. The dreamed meetings end with the fugitive shooting Villari, but no solace or assurance is obtained; the dreamer is left uneasy and must run through the same narrative night after night. In the waking confrontation, Villari is about to shoot the main character as the story ends. The fugitive welcomes this resolution to the burden of life outside the shared matrix. In putting an end to his escape, Villari restores him to the communal network.

"La escritura del Dios" ("The Writing of the God") has a setting uncharacteristic of Borges's fiction: in the aftermath of the Spanish conquest of the Americas. Its narrator and protagonist is an Aztec priest imprisoned by the victors. Not only was Borges reluctant to draw upon the potential subject matter offered by the great, vanished Indian empires, but he could be sarcastically disdainful of those Latin American thinkers and writers who made too much, for his taste, of this material. In this case, though, the text shows that Borges himself had been looking into the indigenous past, with particular attention to the cosmological and religious systems of pre-Columbian Mexico.

The narrator, who has spent years in an unlighted dungeon, has little sensory evidence with which to conduct the search for his vision. Only occasionally does an opened hatch cast light on a small number of objects. His successful investigation, given such meager resources, testifies to the persistent human drive to discover, or create, order and meaning.

The actual method of investigation occupies a prominent place in the account, as it does in many Borges stories. The priest trains himself to concentrate on the visual information he obtains during the brief moments of illumination. He then spends his hours in darkness reconstructing and fixing in his mind what he has seen. This inquiry becomes urgent when the narrator glimpses the imminence of a readable text in the markings on the skin of a jungle cat. By sifting through his memory for items of arcane lore about secret writings (abundantly transcribed into his account) and seeing significant repetitions in the cat's markings, the priest inevitably finds a hidden message from a god.

The revelation, once obtained, proves other than what was originally sought. The narrator had hoped for divine guidance to reverse the effects of the Spanish conquest. After deciphering the markings, he believes himself to possess the ability to turn history around, but declines to exercise it. The secret he has learned is valuable strictly as a conceptual gift transcending any possible concrete action. Its effect on the narrator is to plunge him into a quietism outwardly indistinguishable from his state before attaining enlightenment.

Borges's stories vary considerably in the possible value they assign to the revelations experienced by characters. "The Writing of the God" is one of the most strongly weighted toward a negative assessment of the knowledge revealed to the character. Throughout, there are hints that the narrator's vision is nothing more than a rearrangement of his knowledge of the world providing comfort in his wretched situation.

"Hombre en el umbral" ("Man on the Threshold") is among the very least discussed of Borges's major stories. It is constructed as the fictional illustration of a paradox: the most judicious arbiter in a case may be a madman, that is, a man devoid of judgment.

The context for this notion is an elaborate detective tale set in a Moslem city of colonial India. The narrator is brought in to investigate a case that has everyone concerned baffled. A hated British official has disappeared without clues; each successive Indian brought in for interrogation manages to obscure the matter yet further. The narrator is nearly in despair when he receives, as an anonymous tip, a street address. The house it designates seems to be the site of some great celebration. The narrator begins to converse with the only occupant of the house who pays him any attention, a tiny, ancient man he finds crouched on the threshold. This unpromising informant, who resembles a number of unlikely guides in Borges stories, tells the narrator everything he cares to know and adds his own reflective commentary.

The man on the threshold begins by giving a sober account of the official's kidnapping by an ad hoc guerrilla organization, which then arranges a trial for him. The most difficult procedural point is the designation of a judge. The religious cultures of the subcontinent, which the old man enumerates, all have produced reflective and conscientious representatives. Yet each of them is committed to one perspective to the exclusion of others. At this point the informant mentions, in an unemphatic way, that a naked madman was found to fill the judge's role. The stodgily Western narrator is upset by the solution, but all involved, including the official on trial, have approved of it. The rationale stems from a concept Borges found particularly beautiful: the individual who holds to no particular set of beliefs can represent, or be, either no one or all things. The old man comments that God could speak through the madman. This remark not only evokes the idea that the insane are blessed; it also implies that a demented, denuded, and homeless judge could express a viewpoint transcending that of anyone enmeshed in the outlook and beliefs shared by social groups.

The ending of "Man on the Threshold" leaves the story's time sequence ambiguous. The old man's account of the trial appears to refer to events in the past, but when the narrator leaves him, he encounters the mad, naked judge, brandishing the sword freshly bloodied in carrying out the sentence. One possibility is that the old man has such prescience that he can speak with retrospective certainty of events still under way. Another is that the narrator has entered cyclical time, where successive versions of the official reappear periodically to be hated, kidnapped, judged, and condemned.

"El muerto" ("The Dead Man") foreshadows in its title the unhappy realization that, in the final passage, overtakes the narrator and completely alters the meaning of the story's events. Most of the text is taken up with an anomalous success story. An unremarkable young man, a Buenos Aires street tough, suddenly gains the chance to start life afresh. He joins a band of smugglers and begins to live out adventures in rugged terrain. Most amazingly, he seems to be succeeding in his plan to usurp the head smuggler's commanding position, along with his mistress and his prized horse and saddle trappings. The rapturous tale of endless opportunities comes to a harsh end. The protagonist realizes that he has long been condemned for his undisguised campaign to displace his superior. The smugglers have allowed him to sample the chief's privileges because, being virtually a dead man, he is of no significance.

A set of elements Borges has been reworking since "Streetcorner Man" comes into play in "The Dead Man." The primary focus is on the relations between gang leaders, with their strenuously cultivated dominance, and the rank-and-file members of these associations. Characteristically, Borges shows a street lord or chief outlaw through the eyes of a young subordinate. In the most typical version, the lowly protagonist idolizes the gang leader, then enters into a crisis of disillusionment when his hero reveals inadequacies common among ordinary people. This is an arrangement to which Borges will return in his stories of the late 1960s and 1970s.

In "The Dead Man," the routine hood is concerned not with lionizing but with being the one on top. Nonetheless, this dim, callow character misperceives the way dominance is achieved and maintained. He can always stand out momentarily by displaying his physical courage, and it is the sight of the chief in a moment of apparent physical weakness that makes him think he can replace this longtime leader. He leaves out of account the strategy and calculation required to remain in a position of preeminence.

"La Busca de Averroes" ("Averroes' Search") presents a struggle to wrest unwieldy information into a satisfactorily meaningful configuration. Averroes, the Islamic scholar rediscovering the learning of classical antiquity, is nearly overwhelmed with bewilderment over the translation of Aristotle's terms *comedy* and *tragedy*. Unacquainted with theater, he does not see how Aristotle's words separate two special subclasses of this general phenomenon.

Despite the lack of familiar conceptual landmarks, Averroes manages to produce an explanation of the terms that has enough internal consistency to satisfy him. His solution, which appears transcribed into the text of the story, is certain to strike a modern reader as defective: "Aristu (Aristotle) applies the name of tragedy to panegyrics and the term comedy to satires and anathemas" (*Labyrinths*, 155; *El Aleph*, 100), he says, referring his readers to the Koran for samples of both forms.

Averroes, however, is satisfied with the definition: "Something had revealed to him the meaning of the two words" (*Labyrinths*, 155; *El Aleph*, 100).

This is one of the few cases in Borges in which readers have some way of judging revealed knowledge, since readers have grounds on which to criticize the distinction Averroes has attributed to Aristotle. While contemporary definitions of Aristotelian terms are themselves fallible, a point the story makes, Averroes's are indisputably flawed from the start by his ignorance of theater.

The principal failure the story narrates is Averroes's doomed effort to identify subcategories. All around him events are occurring or being discussed; each bears some relation to his struggle. Wheelock (157–58) observes that each lateral anecdote in some way parallels the protagonist's work to make meanings come clearly into focus as the correct ones. At a party Averroes attends, a guest tells of seeing, while abroad, a drama performed. This account proves incomprehensible to the guests. They have the concept of narrative, but not that of theater, and so cannot grasp why theatrical representation should require a greater number of participants than other ways of telling tales do. Other events are analogous to Averroes's search in less obvious ways. For example, one harem slave is tormented by others, presumably for the anomalous red hair that enables her to claim greater attention. Some boys engage in a game whose rules cause conflict, since only one of the players can hold the desired place of preeminence. In each case, the problem is caused by one of several competing elements prevailing, or seeking to prevail, over the others. The dilemma is inescapably entailed by the basic cognitive need to draw distinctions. The resolution of this issue is always inadequate. In an epilogue, Borges looks back over this tale of faulty discriminations and wonders whether his own effort to imagine Averroes would not reveal itself, in some larger perspective, as equally flawed; he ends by despairing of the possibility of verifying what seems true.

Critical Triumph and the
Return to Tale-telling

While Borges was engaged in the elaboration of the stories that would be deemed his major accomplishment, he took time for a lighter-hearted approach to the form. Sharing the pseudonym H. Bustos Domecq with his collaborator Bioy Casares, Borges created a number of intricate and ingenious variants on the tale of detection. The resulting stories, gathered in the 1942 *Seis problemas para don Isidro Parodi* (*Six Problems for Don Isidro Parodi*, 1981), are amusing but not innocuously so. The convention that detection should be accomplished through sheer force of intellect is here taken to an extreme. Isidro Parodi is like Sherlock Holmes's brother Mycroft, introduced by Sir Arthur Conan Doyle on a few occasions, who was too bulky to investigate crimes, yet could draw powerful conclusions from the scraps of information others brought. In Parodi's case, a prison sentence has immobilized the detective, but he has learned to squeeze insights from severely limited data. This mastermind's name is an accurate sign of the temper of the stories in which he appears. Together with intellectual puzzles and plot twists, they contain acid satire directed against those whose verbal expression, beliefs about art, political views, and personal style were not up to the authors' standards of simple elegance. Both authors were gifted mimics of overly refined speech and of affectations in written style. In addition, there is an at times quite cruel mockery of lower class characters, perhaps a reflection of the exacerbated class antagonism in the years leading up to and running through the regime of Juan Domingo Perón.[12]

During the same period, Borges and Bioy co-edited the 1943 *Los mejores cuentos policiales* (The best detective stories), which displayed the subgenre in its most coolly intellectual forms. This volume was reissued on several occasions, as was a 1951 sequel. The two editors were successful in spreading their enthusiasm for detective stories constructed as an ingenious challenge to the reader's wits. In 1946 Borges and Bioy published, under the joint name B. Suárez Lynch, a capricious long story or short novel called *Un modelo para la muerte* (A model for death). The entire narrative is written in an exaggerated variant of *lunfardo*, a street argot that had been taken up and embellished by local-color writers. This overdone dialect compounds the difficulty of following a detective plot so convoluted as to necessitate some words of guidance from a commentator. The interpreter who steps forward to offer an explanation, however, is another Borges-Bioy invention, and further disorients the reader. This work is notable for showing an almost purely whimsical version of the vertiginously complex Borges world. It is also, at eighty-three not very closely printed pages, as near as Borges comes to authoring a novel. The author frequently expressed a belief that while the novel had once been exciting, unexplored terrain for authors and readers, by now there was little point in running through such a full-scale exercise. This outlook is consistent with Borges's custom of developing only the concepts for possible novels. Rather than elaborate the novels, he would use their premises in describing works attributed to characters in his short stories.

Texts such as these detective tales, ostensibly for entertainment but revealing of matters that preoccupied Borges, are characteristic of work he undertook, at various moments, in forms that did not quite count as his serious writing. In a number of cases these were anthologies or collections of material Borges had gathered and retold in his own distinctive fashion. Collaborators were often involved; when Bioy was not the one to take this role, it was often assumed by one of the literary women with whom Borges enjoyed lengthy friendships. The Argentine literary public followed these digressions with interest, at times using them to second-guess what was really most concerning Borges at a given time. In fact, these minor works can provide clues to the author's shifting enthusiasms. For example, his 1951 *Antiguas literaturas germánicas* (Ancient Germanic literatures; Icelandic verse was the featured topic) mixed popularized scholarship with Borges's ideas on metaphor. Written in collaboration with Delia Ingenieros (and rewritten in 1966 with María Esther Vásquez), it showed Borges struggling for a scholarly grasp of the ancient Nordic cultures frequently mentioned in his work. *Los orilleros; El paraíso de los creyentes* (The denizens of the waterfront; The paradise of believers, 1953), another collaboration with Bioy, was the only attempt at scriptwriting by Borges, an enthusiastic moviegoer; the two film scenarios went unproduced.

During this same period, while his originality and productivity were at their height, Borges's career was frustrated in various ways owing to his much-publicized conflict with the government. The 1946–55 presidency of Juan Domingo Perón, with its mix of populism, social programs, and charismatic rule, failed to win much support among intellectuals. Borges, as an emblem of the anti-Peronist literary elite, became a target of Perón's harassment. He was stripped of his librarian post and appointed an inspector in a public market. His sister was briefly jailed and his mother kept under house arrest. In turn, Borges placed in his writings, particularly in his stories co-authored with Bioy, denigrating but oblique allusions to Perón, his wife, Eva, and their lower class supporters.

In 1955 Perón was deposed. There was a widespread campaign to restore Borges's place in the nation's cultural life. The most important action was his appointment as director of the National Library. Much was made of such events as the 1956 publication of a new edition of *Ficciones* that contained stories written since the 1944 version. Borges and Bioy again flourished as arbiters of taste with such co-edited anthologies as their 1955 *Cuentos breves y extraordinarios* (*Extraordinary Tales*, 1971, translated by Anthony Kerrigan).

The late fifties also saw the beginnings of what would become a flood of Borges criticism. The author was particularly fortunate in having as one of his early critics Ana María Barrenechea. Her 1957 *La expresión de la irrealidad en la obra de Jorge Luis Borges* (an expanded version appeared in English as *Borges the Labyrinth Maker*, 1965) and her teaching demonstrated the possibilities for scholarly analysis of Borges's short stories.[13] Anti-Borges commentary also arose during the late 1950s. This negative criticism, largely internal to Argentina and reflecting that nation's social conflicts, focused on the lack of political awareness in Borges's fiction and his elite affiliation.[14]

The stories of *Ficciones* and *The Aleph* would be the basis for Borges's world reputation, but for this to happen, an international reading public had to discover them. The process began when Borges's influential sponsor, Victoria Ocampo, brought his work to the attention of Roger Caillois and other representatives of the French literary scene who were spending the war years in Buenos Aires. Caillois, in particular, became eager to win a wider readership for the Argentine author's work, and after the war was probably foremost among those sharing their discovery of Borges with the French reading public. Nestor Ibarra, a bicultural French Argentine and longtime disciple of Borges, with P. Verdevoye produced a French version of *Ficciones* (*Fictions*, 1951); Caillois then published *Labyrinthes* (1953), a selection of stories from the two major collections. Borges became a cult figure among postwar French intellectuals; his work was praised and introduced to the public by such powerful cultural leaders as André Maurois. In the more popular forms of intellectual activity, references to Borges proliferated. A famous example was the 1965 *Alphaville*, one of the brooding films of Jean-Luc Godard, which featured a computer quoting at length from Borges. The Argentine reading public has traditionally followed French literary trends, and so Borges's currency in France enhanced his standing at home.

The contention that interest in Borges spread from France to the rest of the Continent and the English-language countries is borne out by the dates of publication of translations. The French had available translations of most of Borges's major works by the end of the 1950s. Borges's work began to appear in translation in the mid-1950s in Italy and Germany and in the early 1960s in Britain and the United States. Moreover, the French literary world's endorsement of Borges was useful in the promotion of his work to new foreign-language readerships. For example, Maurois's essay introducing Borges's short fiction to foreign readers became, in turn, the preface to the 1962 *Labyrinths: Selected Stories and Other Writings* (edited by Donald Yates and James E. Irby and published by New Directions), the miscellaneous anthology that made the Argentine author a cult figure among U.S. literary intellectuals. *Labyrinths* is also valuable for giving a comparative sampler of early English versions of Borges, with their wide range of approaches to the original text; it collects stories that had appeared singly in little magazines and anthologies during the 1950s and early 1960s. Borges's work reached the United States and Britain simultaneously; the English translation of *Ficciones*, edited by Anthony Kerrigan and with the bulk of the translations executed by him, was issued in 1962 by the Weidenfeld publishing house in London and the New York-based Grove Press.

The enthusiasm of foreign critics for Borges's short fiction presents a complex case of cross-cultural literary reception. At times it has consisted in a relatively straightforward admiration for Borges's stories and a desire to understand them on their own terms. An impressive example is that of the U.S. writer John Updike, who in the 1960s promoted Borges despite the scant resemblance between his own approach to literature and that of the Argentine writer (Updike's 1965 *New Yorker* article, "The Author as Librarian," is considered exceptionally significant in attracting U.S. readers).[15] Borges was presented in a tendentious way by critics involved in the development of particular hypotheses about literature or about the nature of intellectual endeavors. Examples of these specialized and selective ways of reading include the comments of the U.S. fiction writer John Barth, who in a much-noted 1967 essay made Borges exemplary of "The Literature of Exhaustion" characteristic of the late twentieth century.[16]

French critics of the structuralist and poststructuralist eras were quick to claim Borges as support for their assertions about the conventional patterns human beings use to organize information, whether that provided by a literary work or knowledge about society and the natural world. A celebrated instance of the latter is the homage the structuralist thinker Michel Foucault makes to Borges in the preface to his 1966 *Les mots et les choses* (*The Order of Things*, 1970).[17] Here Foucault states that the line of thought he expounds in his book arose from his reading of a passage in Borges. Reading Foucault's earlier work, however, makes one suspect that he was already germinating the ideas for the 1966 book when he came upon Borges's words as welcome confirmation. Still, the correspondences between Borges's short stories and structuralist thought are profound and evident, and the structuralists can hardly be faulted for bringing attention to their kinship with an author enjoying such remarkable prestige. While it might be difficult to prove that Borges changed the course of structuralist thought, and while he could not have been influenced by this movement, structuralist critics contributed many illuminating readings of his fiction. David William Foster's "Borges and Structuralism: Toward an Implied Poetics," included in Part 3 of in this volume, looks carefully at this case of parallelism through analyses of selected short stories of Borges.

While the initial effort to show Borges as a figure of structuralist and poststructuralist thought may have been carried out with an at-times-exaggerated zeal, this much-publicized critical tendency had two positive long-term results. First, critics whose knowledge of Borges was more thorough than that of the French theorists were able to adapt the new currents from France in developing their analyses of Borges's fiction. Probably the most noted example is the 1979 *Las letras de Borges* (Borges's literature; the Spanish title can be translated several ways) by the longtime Borges critic Sylvia Molloy, with its considerable debt to the work of Jacques Derrida.[18] Going beyond the specific issue of new French theory, attentive readers of Borges became aware of many far-reaching ways in which his short stories put forward the questions that have proved most troubling to contemporary critical thought. The relation between Borges's texts and the entire climate of recent literary discussion continues to elicit lively commentary and debate.[19]

Another feature of the international reception of Borges's work deserves notice. In Argentina, Borges was first known as a poet and, even after he established himself as a short story writer, he was not exclusively cast in this latter role; the reading public had regular evidence of his continuing work in the essay, literary journalism, and poetry to which he returned at varying intervals. With the exception of the French, who relatively soon had access to a fair portion of Borges's work, foreign readers for some time hardly knew more than the most famous part of Borges's work: his short stories written from the mid-1930s to the early 1950s. At times, brief essays appeared in translation, as those supplementing the stories in the U.S. anthology *Labyrinths*. But typically the essays translated are those closest to Borges's fiction, particularly those treating philosophical hypotheses and statements as if they were literary inventions. Only as publishers abroad began to look for new items for enthusiasts of Borges in translation did his writing in other genres—work less easily recognizable as his—reach foreign publics. Often there was a great lag between the translation of the short stories and of other works, during which time Borges seemed, to many foreign readers, exclusively an author of short stories and of essays nearly classifiable as brief fiction.

Even if Borges's foreign readership sometimes received an incomplete or a partisan view of his accomplishments, there is no doubt that his work had earned him an international standing. The 1961 awarding of the Formentor (International Publishers) Prize, granted by six prestigious European, British, and U.S. publishers, to Borges and Samuel Beckett is often cited as the first definitive sign of Borges's world reputation. The prize, in turn, resulted in the publication of *Ficciones* by the six publishing houses awarding the prize; these editions included the earlier-mentioned Kerrigan version.

An unexpected career as an international lecturer began when, in the fall of 1961, Borges, through the sponsorship of the Edward Laroque Tinker Foundation, spent a semester as visiting professor at the University of Texas at Austin. Having traveled very little since his last European stay some four decades previously, Borges subsequently was much in demand as a visitor to university campuses and as a speaker at conferences of literary scholars. At a more popular level, journalists and representatives of publishers were eager for Borges's presence at events and sought to obtain fresh quotable comments from him. Borges gave every sign of enjoying his fame and even the more absurd aspects of celebrity. He had, however, many strategies for maintaining his privacy and reserve even when his schedule left him little time alone. Interviewers frequently received responses from Borges that proved to be near duplicates of his previous remarks, suggesting that he had learned his public persona as one would a theatrical role.

As Borges's fame spread, based on the complex, intricate stories of his high period, he had already passed through his period of intense concentration on the genre. His 1952 collection *Otras inquisiciones (Other Inquisitions,* 1964) is of essays, continuing the author's habit of discussing philosophical ideas with more regard for their ability to surprise and delight than for their utility in capturing truths.

As was usual with him, Borges continued to publish various items that for one reason or another were not deemed part of his major work. One of these that has particularly captivated readers is the 1957 *Manual de zoología fantástica* (Handbook of fantastic zoology), as it was first titled. This work, which Borges assembled in collaboration with Margarita Guerrero, curiously belongs both to Borges's nonfiction and to his fantastic literature. It playfully mimics the format of a reference volume, with alphabetically ordered entries on creatures who are fantastic in various ways. Some are mythical, such as the centaur, while others, although recognized by science, were in earlier times believed to possess fabulous attributes, such as the panther. Still others arise not from the collective imagination but from the inventive powers of an individual artist. Borges seems to have had an enduring fascination with beings whose traits or existence, even if once common knowledge, now have no place in the inventory of things known. He continued work on the project after its publication and in 1967 produced the lengthier *El libro de los seres imaginarios.* When Norman Thomas di Giovanni, the translator who had become Borges's agent, assistant, and literary companion, began to discuss an English version of this text, the author involved him in fresh research on the topic. Between them they produced a revised and expanded version entitled *The Book of Imaginary Beings* (1969).

During the 1950s Borges worked in poetry and prose with apparently equal willingness. He had developed an understated verse to replace the avant-garde experimentation he now rejected as untrue to the nature of poetic expression. As opposed to the liberty he had advocated in the 1920s, he now believed in a necessary limitation of poetic possibilities; for instance, while any number of metaphors could be elaborated, only a few were worth including in poetry. Borges was also working with shorter and less definitive forms of prose.

Fittingly representative of his interests during this period is the 1960 *El hacedor.*[20] The material in this work was not intended to form a collection. Rather, Borges responded to his publisher's request for a book-length manuscript by assembling recent imaginative writings, divided about equally between prose and poetry.

The short prose pieces are meditations more than narrations. A set of usually paradoxical considerations is expounded to the reader in a voice that would, by some criteria, be considered that of the author himself. As in many of Borges's essays, the speaker reveals himself to be either a theatricalized or a symbolically transformed alter ego of Borges. Yet the situation is unlike that in *A Universal History of Infamy* and other texts wherein Borges presents himself by assuming an awkward, eccentric, or fatuous persona. Here the speaker gives every sign of being a wise observer willing to allow readers a look into such complex matters as the mystery of literary creation. Even though this commentator is insightful and measured in his expression, there are indications that his words should not be trustingly taken as Borges's own. Indeed, the most famous piece in Dreamtigers, "Borges y yo" (first translated as "Borges and I" by Mildred Boyer and then retranslated by Norman Thomas di Giovanni as "Borges and Myself" in *The Aleph and Other Stories*), is distinguished by the elegant twist that discourages the reader from presupposing the author of an essay to be the speaker in that text. A seemingly guileless "Borges" has been complaining of the writer Borges, a false self constantly posing for a desired artistic or rhetorical effect. At the end, though, the self-displaying author Borges appears likely to have taken over the very text purporting to denounce him as an artificer.

Dreamtigers shows Borges moving back away from the short story form. Some of its brief, meditative texts, like "Borges and Myself," at times appear in collections of short stories. Such inclusions really reflect Borges's fame as a short story writer rather than the characteristics of these texts, which have little to narrate. Still, the prose in *Dreamtigers* develops many of the same preoccupations found in Borges's short stories. Among these are the conjunction of features of the essay with those of imaginative writing and the treatment of philosophical problems without advocating solutions.

The prose pieces of *Dreamtigers* are well regarded, but critics discuss them less frequently than the short stories from the major collections.

Except for "Borges and Myself," the reveries and parables of *Dreamtigers* enjoy relatively little individual fame. Occasionally cited is a speculation about Shakespeare to which Borges gave the English title "Everything and Nothing." It encapsulates his idea that the most admirable minds can shift between points of view; in Shakespeare's case, the result is both genius and the loss of any distinctive self. "El simulacro" ("The Sham") is singled out for a different reason; Borges denigrates Juan and Eva Perón by name.

The publication of the English version of *Dreamtigers*, with the prose translated by Mildred Boyer and the poetry by Harold Morland, is notable in two ways. *Dreamtigers* was issued by the University of Texas Press in 1964 together with *Other Inquisitions*, translated by Ruth L. C. Simms. These two works successfully introduced English-language readers to a Borges more varied than the easily recognizable author of the classic short stories of *Ficciones* and *The Aleph*. They were also the last of Borges's books to be published in English by a relatively small-scale publishing operation; it will be remembered that *Labyrinths* and *Ficciones* were produced by New Directions and Grove Press, with their comparatively small lists directed at an intellectual readership. Subsequently, Borges's English editions would be brought out by large trade publishers, especially E. P. Dutton, evidence that his appeal had spread from a scholarly and elite public to a more general one.

By now Borges had left many of his readers perplexed by the great mass of his work, the frequent changes in his approach to literature, and the multiple and diverse judgments he had at various times pronounced on his own writings. He often derided his earlier work and seldom gave much indication of what he considered his major contributions. For these reasons, great interest was aroused by the 1961 publication of his *Antología personal* (*A Personal Anthology*, 1967), in which Borges presented the works by which he wanted to be known. This book showed Borges to be in some ways not so unlike the majority of readers in his preferences. Along with certain of the stories from *Ficciones* and *The Aleph*, the anthology tended to favor short prose essays and poems that displayed Borges's famous preoccupations: parables, varying concepts of time, the fragility of personal identity, and the enigma of literary creation. The anthology also allowed Borges to recognize figures and sources important to the making of his fiction. In this vein, he included essays on the *Beowulf* narrative, representative of his northern European cultural preoccupations, and on Edward FitzGerald, translator of the *Rubáiyát of Omar Khayyám*, which Borges had frequently echoed. Pieces based on Jewish folklore, baroque literature, the Bible, and Dante further acknowledged debts.

Over the next decade, Borges gave the impression of abandoning the short story. His 1964, 1965, and 1969 collections are of verse, interspersed with some brief pieces of poetic prose. When asked about this shift, Borges frequently attributed it to his deteriorating sight. Virtually blind since the mid-1950s, Borges had learned to retain a shorter composition in his memory while revising it to his satisfaction. This explanation, however practical, could not fully account for his unwillingness to work in the short story. Any number of friends and admirers were ready to read to Borges and take his dictation, including his mother, who became legendary for her ambition for and dedication to her son. Moreover, during 1955–70 he composed lectures, prefaces to books, and other occasional pieces at least as lengthy as short stories.

He also continued to elaborate fiction, but always in some special category that would not count as the Borges short story. An example is his imaginative satirical pieces in collaboration with Bioy Casares. The 1967 *Crónicas de Bustos Domecq* (*Chronicles of Bustos Domecq*, 1976), one of their most comical works, pretends to be a collection of essays by the critic Bustos Domecq—as will be recalled, the name Borges and Bioy earlier used as their joint pseudonym. This time, Bustos Domecq is an exemplary fool invented by Borges and Bioy. His eagerness to appear avant-garde having paralyzed his judgment and good sense, Bustos Domecq endorses artistic experiments that are almost certain to strike readers as worthless. The appeal of the book lies, in large part, in the creation of the fatuous Bustos Domecq, who offers his faulty appraisals in a tasteless mixture of critical jargon and "fine writing." Borges and Bioy also shock and amuse with the pointless artistic undertakings their fictional critic accepts. At one point, for instance, he admires paintings hidden under black paint in an avant-garde observance of religious constraints on the making of images. The satire Borges and Bioy direct against experimental art is a knowing one; both authors had begun their literary careers as avant-gardists and moved toward a more classical norm.

Borges's continued production of relatively lengthy works and the creation of Bustos Domecq suggest that he had available assistance to compose short stories and had retained his enthusiasm for the creation of fictional beings and situations. His avoidance of the genre appears more likely to have resulted from the exhaustion of the impulse that had given rise to the stories of his high period. By now the manner and repertory of elements of those texts were instantly recognizable and easy to imitate. It would have been redundant in a sense for Borges to produce more Borges stories in such a well-established mode. In time, the author began to hint that he had not abandoned the short story, but rather refrained from publishing work in this form until he had found a way to do so without repeating himself.

Doctor Brodie's Report and Other Contemporary Stories

Borges's anticipated return to the short story materialized in 1966, when "La intrusa" ("The Intruder") drew somewhat sensational attention as the first new story Borges had released in thirteen years. More stories were published; the frequency of their appearance rose sharply during 1968–70. It was evident that Borges had caught his second wind as a short story writer. These new stories were grouped in the 1970 *El informe de Brodie* (*Doctor Brodie's Report*, 1973), with the exception of two.[21] "Pedro Salvadores" and "El etnografo" ("The Anthropologist" is Norman Thomas di Giovanni's translated title of the latter) had already been collected, amid new poems, in the 1969 *Elegio de la sombra* (*In Praise of Darkness*, 1974).[22] These two stories were much briefer than the others, which may account for their publication in a volume of verse, but they are otherwise similar and should be considered together with the *Brodie* texts.

The new stories were, in some ways, unlike those of Borges's period of most intense involvement with the short story. The author played up the difference by declaring, in a much-cited 1967 interview with César Fernández Moreno, that he was "weary of labyrinths" and determined to limit the complexity of his current short stories.[23] He seemed to be vowing that he would henceforward express himself more plainly, although longtime readers of Borges doubted that he would ever really renounce indirectness and ambiguity. Of course, the more recent stories revealed, with successive rereadings, half-hidden patterns and areas of uncertainty. Yet it is still fair to call them simpler in the sense that the new pieces, unlike the famous stories of the forties, did not overwhelm the reader with a mass of unruly narrative data. The plot lines were quickly discernible, unobscured by the many erudite-sounding annotations and informative embellishments that characterized the Borges story at the height of its complexity. However the differences or similarities between the new and old stories are viewed, it is undeniable that critics have found less material for commentary in the more recent work and that the classical stories continue to be the ones most often referred to and anthologized.

Rather than call the new mode a simplification, many astute readers spoke instead of Borges's emergence as a storyteller. The short stories published between 1939 and 1953 are famously difficult to summarize. The plots contain so many symbolically freighted elements that any paraphrase must, in selecting what is worth relating, become an interpretation and tell readers what to think about the story. Beyond being inevitably tendentious, such summaries are awkward and unwieldy. The stories of the more recent productive period, in contrast, can be retold; paraphrases involve a loss of subtlety but not the need to rework interpretively the original story. In effect, the *Brodie* texts and the fiction from *In Praise of Darkness* resemble tales made to be recounted in the mode of ghost stories or fireside tales. They center on anecdotes inherently worth the telling, as is the case in "El encuentro" ("The Meeting"), an unabashedly spine-tingling tale of old scores being settled from beyond the grave. Here, two great knife duelists, having missed the chance to meet, posthumously animate their weapons into combat. Two drunken young gentlemen, who really wish each other no great ill, are overwhelmed by a sudden urge to fight using these weapons. Although the men are unacquainted with this type of fighting, their weapons hold the skill and strategy needed to bring the duel to a fatal conclusion. Like orally transmitted anecdotes, many of the new stories have well-calculated "punch lines"; the narrator of "The Meeting" ends by suggesting that the knives may come to life again and claim further unwitting victims.

The plot of "Juan Muraña" also turns on a knife charged with posthumous revenge, but this time there is a more prosaic explanation. Juan Muraña, the narrator's uncle, was another expert in knife fighting. After his death in combat, his family falls on hard times. The landlord threatens to evict them, but the fighter's widow is unconcerned, assuring everyone that Juan Muraña would never allow such an indignity. The landlord is murdered before he can move the family out. Sometime later, the widow offers to show Juan Muraña to her nephew and produces, from a special box, the dead man's dueling knife. The nephew concludes that the widow is in a state of dementia and has killed the landlord by her own efforts. Yet none of the facts he presents rules out a fantastic explanation for the murder. The widow's idea that her husband is still present in the knife remains a possibility.

The prefatory material to this story is a comment on the relation between experience and art. Knowing of Borges's great fondness for portraying toughs, an obnoxious acquaintance accuses the writer of lack of contact with his subject matter. This individual feels his life, much rougher than Borges's, better qualifies him to tell the story of a knife-fighting man; besides, he is the nephew of the great Juan Muraña. The bulk of "Juan Muraña" is given as an extended quotation from this self-appointed expert, whose exact words Borges has tolerantly reproduced. Despite his real-world credentials, the nephew's rendering of the tale has no privileged authenticity that would distinguish it from Borges's efforts. Borges observes that Muraña's nephew is relying on art, rather than on the raw experience he cited as his special gift. He employs rhetorical devices easily recognizable to a veteran narrator. The conclusion to which Borges leads the reader is that the person most entitled to narrate a given type of story is not the one who has lived it but the one who knows how to tell it.

Closely related to the concept of objects that play out long-dormant destinies is the idea of remote causation, in which an event continues to produce unexpected repercussions long after it would seem to have been concluded. "La señora mayor" ("The Elder Lady") presents a comical elaboration of this possibility. Its title character is a threadbare aristocrat, by now senile, whose entire importance rests on being the daughter of a heroic participant in a great battle in the Argentine war of independence. Her claim to renown grows as all other such offspring die off, and by her hundredth birthday she is unique in her privileged bond to this celebrated episode in national history. She now commands public attention on such an overblown scale that it proves too much for her. This last turn of events allows the narrator the concluding remark that the last person killed by the famous Independence Battle was an old woman living in contemporary Buenos Aires. Borges's un-malicious humor in this story comes as a surprise to anyone accustomed to his earlier satirical portraits. The family of the elder lady and her fellow citizens are shown with sympathy in their foolish zeal to magnify the importance of an increasingly tenuous connection with a meaning-conferring event.

"El indigno" ("The Unworthy Friend") is one of the most complex of the new stories, beginning with a title that could allude to either of the unhappily paired protagonists. Their relation is of a type that Borges has often represented: the one through whose eyes events are seen is an unimportant gang member, the other a commanding outlaw who excites the underling's admiration, envy, and outraged disappointment. In this case, both are lowly. The subordinate partner is a Jewish adolescent driven to prove himself brave, loyal, and fully Argentine, while his hero turns out to be a secondary figure in a gang of burglars.

Except for a brief preamble, the story of this bond is told by the lesser gang member, who has since become a solid citizen and can comment with insightful detachment on his insecure earlier self. He now sees how he mistook an apprenticeship in crime for admission to a privileged, unquestionably Argentine sphere of camaraderie and physical courage. But the narrator has no definitive explanation for the shift in perception that makes him reject his leader. Possessing secret knowledge of a scheduled burglary, he first makes his leader state his trust in him, then turns informer. When a policeman inquires about his motivation, he cites a desire to be a good Argentine, a variant on his original purpose in joining the criminals. His cooperation with authorities results in his criminal mentor's death. Afterward, he observes that the popular press makes the dead man into the same hero he had once admired.

The peculiarly intimate act of betrayal, a long-standing Borges preoccupation, grows exceptionally complex in this story. At the most obvious level, the mentor proves unworthy of his recruit's expectations, betraying him by offering nothing more glorious than involvement in breaking and entering. The new gang member, entrusted with secrets and with the vital role of lookout, betrays the confidence placed in him. But the question of who is worthy of whom, or what, goes beyond the immediate events. The protagonist, self-conscious about his Jewishness and timidity, feels less than deserving of full status as an Argentine, which he acritically associates with bold, lawless toughness but also with being a law-abiding citizen. Implicated in the issue of worthiness is the question of hero worship; both the protagonist and the general public idolize individuals who do not merit their admiration.

"El duelo" ("The Duel") is further evidence of a newly subdued approach on Borges's part. Its titular event is a lifelong rivalry that gives two women painters their reason to keep working and, in effect, to continue living. The narrator takes pains to show the respect and affection between the two competitors. Equally evident is his generous outlook toward both of them and his desire to defend them against any suspicion that they may have been mere society belles cultivating ladylike accomplishments. Even the peculiar workings of the art world are shown with good humor, startlingly unlike the sour mockery Borges and Bioy had expressed in *Chronicles of Bustos Domecq*.

"El otro duelo" ("The End of the Duel") follows "The Duel" and serves as a counterbalance to its gentility. Its rivals are two knife fighters who, though they meet in combat, can never kill each other, because their rivalry enlivens their tedious existences. These two fight side by side in Argentina's internal conflicts, though not on speaking terms, and are captured and condemned together. The presiding officer, aware of their legendary competition, gives them one last chance to vie by having them run a race with their throats slit. The seedy fighters are among the most inglorious, banal, and unsympathetic thugs Borges has ever shown, suggesting, as do other elements in contemporary stories, a growing repugnance toward the cult of physical courage.

"Historia de Rosendo Suárez" ("Rosendo's Tale") seconds this note of weariness. The title character is the same tough whose apparent sudden failure of nerve triggered the events of "Streetcorner Man," Borges's first story. Now the author meets his old character, who complains he was misrepresented, although he does not dispute the account of the outward facts. Borges good-naturedly allows Rosendo to tell his story in his own words. According to Rosendo, in the period before the episode described in the story he had been revolted by the pointless fighting and killing around him. He walked away from a challenge so that he could start afresh and has since lived a quiet and orderly life, with which he is content.

The oblique, understated "Pedro Salvadores" is one of the very short stories that appeared in *In Praise of Darkness*. Like most of the fiction from this era, it is purportedly a found, rather than an invented, account. The title character is an undistinguished nineteenth-century liberal until government persecution forces him to spend nine years hidden in the cellar of his house. Most of the narrative appears straightforwardly informative, filled with the specifics of the operations of a household with one of its members concealed under the floorboards.

These details are worthy of attention, but obviously cannot constitute the main point of the story. A more significant theme is introduced through brief and cryptic references. The narrator wonders whether Salvadores, in hiding, had not acquired a certain divinity, and notes that he emerged bloated and never again spoke at a normal volume. The suggestion is that Salvadores has become illuminated in a way impossible for those who remain in contact with society. Although his immobility accounts rationally for his puffiness, the reference to his possible divinity makes his new appearance seem also a sign of a mysterious fullness of knowledge. These few cryptic allusions hint at one of the most unknowable revelations experienced by any Borges character.

"The Anthropologist," also from *In Praise of Darkness*, combines a tale of privileged knowledge with a satire of academic life. Its protagonist is a graduate student in anthropology, Fred Murdoch, who seems to be the proverbial blank slate. A professor, evidently struck by Murdoch's malleability, sends him on a stint of fieldwork too arduous for the older man. If he can learn the initiation secrets of a North American Indian tribe, Murdoch will receive a degree, the university press will score a coup with the publication of his discovery, and the mentor will undoubtedly benefit as well.

During his two years of fieldwork, Murdoch becomes imbued with tribal thought. He is judged fit for initiation and comes into possession of the secret. On his return to campus, he refuses to divulge the knowledge. He is resolved to live in accordance with what he has learned, and presumably does so, although the only outward sign of his transformation is a move from anthropology to library work.

The magical element in "The Anthropologist" is one that repeatedly attracted Borges during this period: unresolved conflicts from the past erupting into the present to influence events. Murdoch had an ancestor who died fighting Indians; he is aware of this ancestral link to his current efforts. As his mind becomes attuned to the tribe's outlook, he dreams of buffalo, an image reminiscent of the destruction of the Great Plains buffalo herds and the federal government's confiscation of tribal lands. An inverse symmetry is created between the ancestor's struggle to expropriate what the tribes once owned and Murdoch's small victory in halting further raids on the indigenous heritage.

In "Guayaquil," a battle of wits is seen from the perspective of the only-partially-resigned loser. The narrator-protagonist, whose historical specialization is unmistakably Argentine, is outmaneuvered by an international investigator known for his scrupulous detachment from the particularistic biases of more rooted scholars. The prize in dispute is the opportunity to examine fresh evidence concerning one of the great puzzles in Spanish-American history. The historical problem, involving the competition for leadership of the wars of Independence, is strongly hinted to be a duplicate of the struggle between the scholars.

The victory occurs through some inner movement so subtle that it represents a mystery as deep as the historical one. Both competitors are struck by a feeling that something inexplicable has occurred, and the international scholar leaves with the remark that the Argentine must have harbored a will to lose. The narrator tactfully abstains from overtly interpreting the events, but by now has given readers enough information to draw further conclusions. If he was driven to defeat by an inherent urge, then the newly discovered evidence will not be able to illuminate the historical problem. The revolutionary who withdrew from the leadership was surely impelled by an analogous will toward defeat, too impalpable to be verified by the scholarly examination of documents.

"The Intruder" has a particular importance as the first example of Borges's new fiction to reach the public. The initial reaction was often one of disappointment; no doubt many readers were expecting Borges to resume the series of stories that occupy *Ficciones* and *The Aleph*. Eventually the tale won greater acceptance, becoming one of the relatively few Borges stories to be adapted to film.

The spectacularly tough world of machismo had long interested Borges, both for an element he admired, physical courage, and for traits he criticized, such as the emphasis on dominating others and on display and posturing. "The Intruder" stresses the negative side of the phenomenon, as Borges became increasingly apt to do in his late fiction. The protagonists are two brothers who, though their standards of masculinity forbid them to concede importance to women, both fall in love. Even worse, they are both obsessed with the same woman and end up sharing her. This arrangement is too unsettling to their relationship and, eventually, one of them feels driven to kill the woman. The narrator concludes that the brothers, who embraced over the woman's death, were now more solidly bonded than ever.

The narrator of "The Intruder" is plainly disapproving of the actions he relates. He points out that the woman entangled in this fraternal drama is treated as "no more than an object" (*Doctor Brodie's Report*, 65; *El informe de Brodie*, 18); she is, at various times, lent and sold, and she is unconsulted and uninformed about her fate. Even more explicitly noted is the macho's exclusive preoccupation with other men; the brothers' great concern is that attachment to the woman will damage their relations with neighborhood men and the ties between them. Grounds are given for the conjecture that the protagonists are incestuously linked, though the narrator limits himself to noting "the close ties between them" (*Doctor Brodie's Report*, 64; *El informe de Brodie*, 17).

"Doctor Brodie's Report" is presented as an old document that has recently been discovered, missing the very page that seems to specify the locale in which it is set. The author is a nineteenth-century Scottish missionary whose work took him among the Mlch tribe. In disgust with what he sees as their coarse ways, Brodie calls the Mlch Yahoos, after the degenerate race in Jonathan Swift's *Gulliver's Travels*. Readers, though, are likely to perceive the Presbyterian minister as unduly severe toward the Mlch. Brodie disapproves of the tribe's hygiene and sexual customs; moreover, he has not been able to make a single convert during his stay. Although the missionary sets out to describe a people poorly developed in their higher faculties, the result is a portrait of abnormally ethereal beings. The paradox, which Brodie gives occasional signs of grasping, is that the Mlch live crudely because they maintain their awareness at such a high level of abstraction. The Mlch, like the people of Tlön, exemplify the application of idealism to everyday existence.

The Mlch do not clutter their minds with details. As a result, they cannot count above four, preferring to carry out their business dealings with laborious repetition rather than encumber themselves with the specifics of numerical systems. Memory is poorly developed, but the Mlch, because they perceive all events as already recorded in the divine mind, have a certain amount of future vision. They give little thought to their living conditions; the missionary is unable to persuade them to move to a nearby, more healthful habitat. The highest good is to keep one's thoughts free of the details of the concrete world; consequently, Mlch kings are blinded and castrated, and their hands and feet amputated.

The missionary comes closest to understanding the Mlch when he describes their idealistic and abstract language. He recognizes that its dominant feature is an extreme reliance on the user's ability to form and recognize generalizations. For example, the monosyllable that signals the feature of dispersion or spottedness can designate the stars, a leopard, or smallpox, as well as a disorderly retreat. These are not metaphorical extensions of the term; an equally primary meaning is involved in each case.

Apart from the fascination of working out the possible results of idealism taken literally, "Doctor Brodie's Report" offers a comical but sympathetic look into a mind torn with ambivalence. Brodie states that he felt disgust at the Mlch, but was won over by their great facility with abstractions and by the evidence that they had once had a writing system. He seems not to suspect that the Mlch have evolved as they have because of, rather than despite, their gift for high-level thought. Brodie fights alongside the Mlch against their enemies and, as it turns out, the purpose of his entire account is to plead with the British Crown for military assistance to the tribe. Yet even in making the case for the Mlch, he cannot help mentioning the horror he experiences at the thought of them.

Although it is easy to link "Doctor Brodie's Report" with "Tlön, Uqbar, Orbis Tertius," the later story is notably more lighthearted. Many attributes of the Mlch tribespeople are essentially jokes; for example, their future vision is so short that they can only foretell such matters as upcoming harassment by a fly or a bird's call. While Borges had been noted for the ominous tone of his references to sexuality, "Doctor Brodie's Report" derives jocular humor from the Presbyterian pastor's unease at the sexual mores of the tribe.

In considering why the new fiction seems so different, it is useful to note a shift, affecting most of the stories, in the representation of conflict. The stories of *Ficciones* and *The Aleph* convey, among other things, a sense that enmity and treachery are everywhere. The characters frequently conspire against one another with elaborate persistence, luring their enemies into various forms of the labyrinth or enmeshing them in sequences of events that will eventually destroy them. In comparison, most of the rivalries shown in the stories of 1966–70 are relatively straightforward and uncomplicated by malice; some of them are benign, though the characters still depend on competition to give meaning to their actions.

Equally telling is the change in the type of settings employed. Borges readers had come to expect crime-ridden slums, entrapping constructions, fatal deserts, and dingy red chambers, as well as such unique scenes as the horribly rebuilt City of the Immortals. Even more ordinary milieus contained grounds for terror, such as the abominable mirror that spies on the characters in the foreboding opening passages of "Tlön, Uqbar, Orbis Tertius."

While seedy environments still appear in the new stories, a new type of backdrop is also in evidence, sometimes in direct juxtaposition to harsh settings: pleasant surroundings that in some way bring the characters solace. The family home of the elder lady bespeaks a loyal effort to preserve a genteel sanctuary despite evidently encroaching shabbiness. The narrator of "The Unworthy Friend" tells, from the refuge of his successful bookstore, of his brief criminal career. The main narrative of "The End of the Duel" takes place in rough circumstances, but Borges remarks, in a preamble, that a friend told him the story one leisurely summer afternoon in Adrogué, an area famous for its large, beautiful vacation houses. Even Rosendo Juárez, once a dancehall brawler, has moved to the most peaceful neighborhood he can afford. These and other similar indications made some Borges readers feel the author was losing his fire, while others simply noted a shift in the outlook reflected in his fiction.

Nonetheless, Borges's work of 1966–70 was not unfailingly distinguishable from his writing of the *Ficciones* and *Aleph* collections. "El evangelio según Marcos" ("The Gospel according to Mark"), for example, is as ominous as the earlier stories. A student spends time with a family that has some Scottish Calvinist ancestry but no conscious familiarity with Christian thought. The family members have regressed into uncommunicative illiteracy; the student engages their interest with Gospel readings, but then discovers that they have taken the Crucifixion story as a plan for action. The story opens many possibilities for interpretation (see, for example, Wheelock's analysis of "Gospel" as an allegory concerning readers and the text, reprinted in an article in Part 3 of this volume).

"The Gospel according to Mark" exemplifies the way that Borges's late stories reflect on his earlier ones by reiterating certain of their features in altered form. Consider such charged details as the association of English-language culture with primitivism, which draws attention to the many times Borges has linked it to cultivation and even a weary hypercivilization. Borges had often shown bizarrely convoluted interpretations of sacred texts and the erudite sophistication of theologians. "The Gospel according to Mark" explores the converse. The most basic and unelaborated of the Gospels comes in for a reading that is stunning in its crude literalism.

Magic and Nostalgia: *The Book of Sand*

"El Congreso" ("The Congress") was published in a separate volume in 1971 and reissued in Borges's last independently authored volume of short stories, the 1975 *El libro de arena* (*The Book of Sand*, 1977).[24] The Congress of the World is another conspiracy that, as described here, is so vast and subtle that it need hardly even exist. The narrator recounts his involvement in the enterprise and its gradual evolution into a state indistinguishable from simple dissolution.

Great importance is given to the exact composition of the Congress. Recruitment of new members has as its goal the perfect representation of all human groups. Initiates from diverse ethnic backgrounds, religions, and occupations are duly admitted, but the success of the plan is impossible to evaluate. The multiple nature of all things makes representivity elusive, since each human being carries many identity traits and may be considered to exemplify many different aggregations. A related problem complicates efforts to amass a documentary archive: no item, however ephemeral, may be excluded in favor of others.

Equally troublesome is the nature of the group's endeavor. The members are so intent on preserving an all-inclusive grand scope for their project that any specific plan for action threatens to become reductive. Whether despite or because of this vagueness, the organization's business proceeds at a bustling pace; the narrator finds himself caught up in a packed schedule of events, his Congress duties bring travel and romance, the latter narrated in a lyrical erotic prose that has no precedent in Borges's work.

The activity comes to a halt when the president of the Congress, following a sudden insight, orders its dissolution. He has seen the Congress of the World as absolutely coterminous with the world. His colleagues grasp this point and become as zealous in their disunity as they once were in banding together; if their paths cross, they either discuss other matters or give no signs of recognizing one another. The parting suggestion is that everyday life constitutes the workings of the congress.

The Book of Sand did not stir as much excitement as *Doctor Brodie's*

Report. It resembles its predecessor volume in the emphasis on story-telling, the clear and easily summarizable plot lines, and the frequency with which supernatural phenomena figure in the narratives. Borges's fascination with the north of Europe, particularly Scotland, Ireland, and Scandinavia, is again allowed to come to the fore, as is his fondness for the mimicry of archaic styles. The use of aged narrators is of particular concern in many of the stories. On the one hand, these old men are privileged witnesses to extraordinary events, including those which required years to develop. On the other, the faculty of memory, which provides these narrators' special claim on listeners' attention, itself becomes the object of anxious and suspicious inquiry.

The title story features another of the objects that come into the lives of Borges characters and succeed in disturbing their usual patterns of understanding the world. In this case, as in many others, the charged item is a book, "of sand" by virtue of its shifting, multifarious character. The book is in a script unrecognizable to the narrator, but its Arabic numerals bespeak its earthly origin and thoroughgoing strangeness; its pagination is wildly discontinuous. The peculiar salesman who has brought this object to the narrator now challenges him to turn to the first and last pages. In either case, more and more leaves interpose themselves; infinity of space and time are among the properties of this object.

The salesman agrees to barter away this book with a readiness the narrator later comes to understand. While possessing the all-inclusivity of the Aleph, the object is a Zahir, capable of completely dominating the thoughts of its owner. Some of Borges's most vivid writing of his late period is found in the narrator's account of his obsession. Although the book torments him with its infinity, what he most dreads is either losing it or discovering it to be finite. He reports ending his ordeal by leaving the book randomly placed in the stacks of the National Library, of which, of course, the real-life Borges was long the director.

Borges opens interpretive possibilities by giving his own book the name used for the imaginary work. In a sense, the Book of Sand is the ideal book to author, even if it is a terrible one to own. Borges has often considered the powerful desire to represent all of everything; his characters become consumed with the struggle toward the total work of art or thought. Also among Borges's themes is the compulsion, common among authors, to intrigue and captivate. The Book of Sand, which contains all of time and space and has a limitless ability to command attention, can be seen as the fulfilment of writers' strivings, though not of their most worthy ones.

"El espejo y la máscara" ("The Mirror and the Mask") gives a more noble image of devastating and ultimate creation. This account, in archaic style, of the search for beauty through poetry begins with the High King of Ireland commanding the court bard to sing of his exploits in battle. The poet first produces skillful, conventional heroic verse; he earns a silver mirror. He later wins a golden mask with an unusual, evocative piece. The next time, he has the king clear the room before reciting his poem. It is a single line whose beauty, being absolute, is sinful for human beings to perceive. The bard is rewarded with the means to commit suicide and the king becomes a vagabond penitent.

The bard's successive efforts have a significant resemblance to Borges's often-reconsidered poetics. The second poem is described in terms unmistakably reminiscent of avant-garde poetry, in which the young Borges placed great hopes. The poet's earliest attempt, which honors convention, corresponds well to Borges's middle years, when he began advocating greater reliance on the poetic past. The third poem comes to the bard as revealed knowledge, but to maintain its purity he must have the aesthetic good judgment to refrain from embellishment. This restraint on the part of an eloquent poet speaks well for minimalism. In making the poet's greatest achievement also his most taciturn, Borges defends the ideal of simplicity and understatement that he strives for in his last years.

One theme of "The Mirror and the Mask," the terror of going beyond the usual human limitations, is presented with lurid Gothicism in "There Are More Things" (original title in English). Dedicated to H. P. Lovecraft, the American master of chilling tales, this story centers on an ancestral home that has fallen into the hands of alarming strangers. The narrator comes back from advanced study abroad to discover his uncle's familiar house undergoing transformations. Local informants express apprehension, but fall silent when the narrator asks for particulars. The centerpiece of the tale is an account of a stealthy tour of the house, whose furniture is obviously designed to accommodate bodies far from the human pattern. With a macabre showiness suitable to the "cruel tale," the account breaks off just as the narrator is about to behold one of the beings to whom the house is tailored.

Despite the urgency of his story, the narrator takes the opportunity to meditate further on the nature of perception. Many items in the house are impossible for him to describe because they correspond to nothing in his experience. In other cases, he can offer analogies, such as an operating table or a trough, to try to evoke the disturbing furniture. The effort to reconstruct the shape of the inhabitants is wrenching because it goes against the narrator's accustomed categories for making sense of the visible world.

"Undr," set in a vaguely ancient Scandinavia, centers on a search for the absolute word. The quest story is elaborately framed; a modern narrator presents a recently discovered manuscript, whose author speaks at length before beginning the real story, as told him by an aged roving poet. This man set out, long before, to find the land of the Urns, where poetry consisted of one word. On his arrival, he witnessed an utterance of the word, though the exact lexical item escaped him. After many years of seeking, he believes that he knows the word, and so returns to the land. There he reencounters a fellow bard who had earlier befriended him and who is now in his last moments of life. The dying poet is eager to know whether the pilgrim's revelation was valid. He sings to him with one word, and the traveler satisfies his expectations by singing back with a different one.

An intricate matter in "Undr" is the degree to which the secret of the word is, in fact, hidden. On the one hand, the protagonist is told that his life is in danger as a result of having heard the word pronounced. Yet as the ending reveals, the precise word used was not important. The first Urn the narrator meets is a peasant, who is barred from the hall where the word will be uttered. This lowly man, though disingenuously protesting his ignorance of the matter, reveals an understanding of the variable nature of the word when he points out several diverse objects as its manifestations. The clues could indicate that a display of secrecy is made to mislead outsiders into searching for a specific password; Urns know that many words, or perhaps any, will work. This and other related questions remain unanswered in the equivocal and cryptic tale.

"Avelino Arredondo" is an imaginative re-creation of the hidden life of the man who, in 1897, assassinated the president of Uruguay. Borges states plainly that his version of this historical event is his own fantasy of how it might have been. His Avelino Arredondo is determined to kill the president on the grounds that he has proved unworthy of his party's ideals. In short, this is another tale of betrayal and its aftermath.

The most striking portion of this story, one of Borges's most subdued, describes Arredondo's two-month retreat to prepare himself for his deed. The rationale for the withdrawal is not divulged until the end, though the assassin's self-enclosure in a far room of his house is evidently a rite of purification. After the assassination, Arredondo explains that he wanted to avoid implicating his friends, fiancée, and even journalists who, had he read their work, might be said to have influenced him. In this way, the act intended to remedy betrayal is kept uncontaminated by betrayal.

"El soborno" ("The Bribe") is, in the usual manner of fiction with an academic setting, full of machinations and one-upmanship. Of two experts in early Germanic languages, only one can be chosen to present a paper at a conference. One of their departmental colleagues must make the selection. The one who wins this privilege has, during the period of decision, published an article complaining of teaching practices that are obviously those of the man who is evaluating him. After the decision is announced, the winner visits the scholar who selected him and proudly reveals his strategy. He rushed the article into print knowing it would spur the offended party to demonstrate his fair-mindedness by, in effect, rewarding his attacker.

"La noche de los dones" ("The Night of the Gifts") is an example of the use Borges made of aged narrators whose memories, by extending far into the past, continue to generate fresh complexities. Here, the ancient speaker is noncommittally introduced by a younger one, who seems unwilling to intrude on the older man's special relationship with the past.

This elderly Argentine provides a link with the country's frontier days, summed up in the legendary outlaw Juan Moreira. He enters an abstract discussion of Platonic archetypes, claiming, with feigned modesty, that he can tell only a specific tale, a reminiscence of the night he saw Moreira die. On the same night, he heard a woman relate how she was taken captive by Indians. Of course, Borges's story is far from plain; it turns out to be an original commentary on the question of archetypes.

The crucial problem of the story emerges from the parallelism between the woman with her tale of marauding Indians and the man with his eyewitness account of Moreira's death. The man recognizes that the woman constructs a special meaning for herself around the extraordinary experience of captivity, and now he finds himself drawn into the same pattern of behavior as one of the witnesses to Moreira's death. Memories of such monumental events are particularly suspect. The man realizes that his memories of Moreira are ineluctably merged with the popular image of the bandit; Moreira's story has been continuously dramatized and illustrated. Moreover, even memories that seem to be his own may not be firsthand, but rather the effect of remembering his earlier accounts of events. The result is a composite, communal image far removed from fresh experience, perhaps one of the Platonic archetypes that had been under discussion.

The old man is resigned to the idea that he cannot count his memories as his own. The unstable, collectively constructed nature of knowledge proves reassuring once he understands the permeability of the individual. Memories that draw on the experience of all are, for him, the true gifts. The accepting attitude of this late Borges character contrasts with the anxiety earlier figures express over the same issues; consider the narrator of "The Aleph" with his desperate campaign to preserve memory against erosion and contamination.

"El disco" ("The Disk") appears as the autobiographical account of a peasant living somewhere in Scandinavia during the times when Christianity coexisted with the worship of Nordic divinities. The decisive event in his life was a meeting with an old man who carried in his clenched hand a disk belonging to Odin and conferring kingship on the bearer. The disk reveals its divine origin by having only one side. The most original passages in this story describe, in the words of the simple protagonist, that profoundly strange object. The story ends on the moralistic note characteristic of fairy tales: the greedy peasant kills the bearer of the disk and forever after is tantalized by the proximity of the divine object, which nonetheless eludes him.

While Borges has often written of objects that come into characters' lives to torment them, "The Disk" stands out among such tales by the extreme primitivism of the narrator. This dull-witted individual fails to register wonder at the disk, which appears to him a salable treasure; he displays no guilt over murdering its bearer; and he does not suspect that his obsession may be a form of divine or cosmic retribution. "The Disk" illustrates the new minimalism that upset many Borges readers who had especially prized his work for its baroque intricacy.

"La secta de los Treinta" ("The Sect of the Thirty") takes up again the heretical worship of Judas, the theme of "Three Versions of Judas." This time Borges gives it a crude, unvarnished treatment. A brief note prefaces an imaginary document by an enemy of the sect, a single-minded investigator concerned only with excoriating this outbreak of deviance.

The heretics of the Thirty view all those involved in the Crucifixion as involuntary participants, merely borne along by events, with the exception of Jesus and Judas, the prime movers in the drama. These two are worshiped equally; a Temple of the Thirty Pieces of Silver was, according to the narrator, the source of the sect's name. This deviant theology is accompanied by an understanding of the Scriptures so literal as to verge on the comic. Since inward lust is equated with adultery, the sectarians assume that everyone is already guilty of this sin; therefore, no one can be singled out for any special sexual misconduct and all types of sexual expression are permissible. Like the Guthries of "The Gospel according to Mark," the followers of the heresy maintain the practice of crucifixion.

In the course of investigating the sect's aberrations, the narrator has come to share at least one of these, an understanding of the sacrifice of Jesus as theater. He is suspiciously adept at conveying the vision of the Crucifixion as a spectacle meant to convince through dramatic rhetoric. Later, he apologetically finds himself referring to the execution as a tragedy. The implication is that the heretical thought of the Thirty has already begun to exercise a pull on him. The manuscript breaks off just as the panic-stricken narrator is calling on both earthly and heavenly forces to exterminate the heretics.

"El otro" ("The Other") recounts a meeting taking place on a park bench that is somehow both in Cambridge, Massachusetts, in 1969 and in Geneva in 1918. On it are the old Borges and his young self. The young Borges is unnerved by the encounter, which he attempts to rationalize as a dream. More specifically, he wants it to be his dream, with the old man merely a character in it. His older counterpart has long accepted the unreal as an inherent component of everyday life and has no fear of discovering himself either a dreamer or the dreamed-of party. To convey this relativism to the apprehensive young man proves an impossible task. The story, like others of this period, assigns resignation and tranquility to the mature. An anxious striving for control over one's personal reality and a need to determine the exact nature of events typify the young.

Although "The Other" is more of an occasion for reflection than a fantastic story, Borges has been scrupulous in observing many of the conventions of the time-travel narrative. For example, careful attention goes to the specific mechanisms involved. The young Borges raises such questions as "If you have been me, how do you explain the fact that you have forgotten your meeting with an elderly gentleman who in 1918 told you that he, too, was Borges?" (*The Book of Sand*, 17; *El libro de arena*, 11–12). It is a concrete detail—a date printed on a banknote, when paper money ought to be undated—that allows Borges to develop, in retrospect, an explanation of the encounter.

"Utopía de un hombre que está cansado" ("Utopia of a Tired Man") is squarely in the tradition of utopian fiction. The narrator tells of his brief journey to a future where the problems of present-day society have been remedied. Some of the reforms are fairly conventional, such as the abolition of money, private possessions, poverty, and unemployment. World harmony has increased with the substitution of Latin for national languages, and governments are no longer needed. To these unsurprising improvements are added more startling ones arising from Borges's specific concerns.

Life in this future, as in Tlön and the land of the Mlch, is based on idealistic principles. Specific items of information are considered to impede thought, and so schools teach "doubt and the art of forgetting" (*The Book of Sand*, 91; *El libro de arena*, 83). Many individuals have no personal name. To curb the proliferation of needless books and the consequent sense of overload, printing is banned. A book must now be worth the effort of copying out. Simply reading a work is not considered a very high level activity. More value is placed on rereading, in which the rough work of obtaining and assembling data can take second place to the refinements of analysis and reflection. Borges's habit of reading philosophy as imaginative writing seems now to be the normal practice; his host in the future un-self-consciously identifies the *Summa Theologica* as a fantastic narrative.

The hint contained in the title is taken up again in the last section of the story. In this utopia, there is a widespread admission that life is not necessarily worth carrying on. Each man fathers only one child; nothing is said of mothers, an omission that hints at some variant mode of reproduction. A movement is under way to replace this slow attrition of human life with mass suicide. In the meantime, individual suicide is the normal form of death. An adult, which is to say anyone over a hundred, chooses when to go to a public facility for euthanasia. The narrator is on hand when his host enters the crematorium, coolly taking his leave of the friends who have come to see him off. The traveler, himself an elderly man, is fascinated by this scene. The story ends by observing a venerable convention of fantastic travelogues. The narrator is now home, meditating on his experiences; their reality is bolstered by the presence of an object brought back from the world just visited.

Perhaps the greatest surprise to longtime Borges readers was "Ulrica" ("Ulrike"; Norman Thomas di Giovanni's translation, realized in consultation with Borges, restyles the titular heroine's name to a form more distinctive to the Germanic languages). This story is presented as a reminiscence of an encounter with a young Norwegian woman. The mysterious Ulrike offers herself to the Colombian professor who narrates the story, and he gratefully accepts. The eroticism of "Ulrike" surprised readers, not by any raw frankness but by its lyricism and the narrator's good will toward Ulrike and her gift of herself, which he considers welcome and comforting. Borges had occasionally touched on sexual matters in his stories, but often in their most sinister aspects. In his stories of Buenos Aires lowlife, he had stressed the pathological machismo of small-time gangsters and the sexual subjugation of their molls and prostitutes. One of the most famous lines in Borges is a Tlön maxim that first appears misquoted as "mirrors and copulation are abominable" (English *Ficciones*, 17; Spanish *Ficciones*, 13). The one scene of sexual activity found in the short stories, in "Emma Zunz," from *The Aleph*, gave further reason to believe that sexuality was a malignant force in Borges's fictional world. Here the heroine's deflowering is a ritual of degradation. "Ulrike" is in a sense a reworking of the sexual episode from "Emma Zunz," which also involves an isolated sexual encounter with a stranger whose otherness is increased by a distinctly Nordic appearance. While the foreigners and strangers in "Emma Zunz" have no common language and no curiosity about one another, in "Ulrike" they are able to establish a certain understanding despite the limited extent of their acquaintance. Ulrike is an enigmatic but not a disturbingly hermetic and opaque figure.

The Book of Sand was Borges's last set of stories. His further original, single-authored work consisted of four poetry collections. Borges, who had at various times composed verse in English, now virtually became an English-language poet by working closely with his current translator into that language, the poet Alastair Reid. *La rosa profunda* (1975) means "the deep rose"; Borges and Reid agreed to *The Unending Rose* for the English-language selection from this volume included in *The Gold of the Tigers: Selected Later Poems* (1977). *La moneda de hierro* (1976; The iron coin), *Historia de la noche* (1977; A history of night), and *La cifra* (1981; The cipher), the final collections Borges published, take his verse further toward plain expression and understatement. A number of the late poems appeared in English within a short time of their original composition; Borges and Reid had such visible outlets as the London *Times Literary Supplement* and the *New York Review of Books*.

His other late books were a miscellany. Only marginally in the category of narrative is *Libro de sueños* (Book of dreams) of 1976, which tells the plots of dreams by others and, in some cases, of Borges's own. The selection of dreams is plainly based not on their content or significance but on their value as enigmatic tales. Borges, who was skilled at retelling a plot in such a way as to interpret it, here is blankly noncommittal in presenting his material.

Bioy Casares and Borges collected their most recent fiction in collaboration in *Nuevos cuentos de Bustos Domecq* (Bustos Domecq's new stories, 1977). Unlike the earlier *Chronicles of Bustos Domecq*, these stories are not the fashionable nonsense produced by H. Bustos Domecq in his role as chic art critic. Instead, Bustos Domecq now specializes in listening to and transcribing anecdotes told to him by his colorful acquaintances. His informants are shrewd, if not very educated, observers of life in working-class Buenos Aires. The notion that Borges had become more benevolent in his authorial stance toward humankind receives support from this volume. The characters that appear in these stories often engage in elaborate rivalries and feuds, but they are winsome and amusing. Borges and Bioy, who could be cruel in their imitations of lower class speech, here merely show it as picturesque. The artless-looking illustrations by Fernández Chelo, which nostalgically portray Buenos Aires uncontaminated by mass media and the detritus of a big city, intensify the sunniness of these late stories.

During the remaining years of his life, Borges continued to arouse interest and, in the case of his statements on political matters, polemic. In his still-frequent interviews, he passed judgment, sometimes thoughtful and sometimes mischievous, on literary figures and movements. His lengthy and profound involvement with Buenos Aires literary life made him a valuable witness to those periods now beginning to fade into oblivion. Borges had an exceptional memory for the details of everyday life in the early twentieth century, a faculty he used to his advantage in interviews. Although he was still able to command attention and to provoke widespread amusement and indignation, Borges did very little new writing after 1981. Although frail for many years, however, Borges did not begin to withdraw from the literary scene until well into the 1980s. He returned to Geneva, where he had spent much of his adolescence, and died there in 1986.

Notes to Part 1

1. Martin S. Stabb, *Jorge Luis Borges* (New York: St. Martin's Press, 1970); hereafter cited in the text.

2. The information about Borges's earliest readings and writings comes from his "An Autobiographical Essay" in *The Aleph and Other Stories, 1933–1969, Together with Commentaries and an Autobiographical Essay*, ed. and trans. Norman Thomas di Giovanni (New York: E. P. Dutton, 1970), 203–60; hereafter cited in the text as *The Aleph and Other Stories*. This essay appeared originally in English, presented in both the *New Yorker* and the anthology cited here. The same text is the source for the somewhat dramatized account Borges liked to give of his delayed flowering as a short story writer. The critic who has most explored the background behind the statements Borges makes in this essay is Emir Rodríguez Monegal in his *Jorge Luis Borges: A Literary Biography* (New York: E. P. Dutton, 1978); hereafter cited in the text.

3. Edna Aizenberg, "A Vindication of the Kabbala," in her *The Aleph Weaver: Biblical, Kabbalistic and Judaic Elements in Borges* (Potomac, Md.: Scripta Humanistica, 1984), 85–107; hereafter cited in the text.

4. Jaime Alazraki, "Borges and the Kabbalah," *TriQuarterly* 25 (1972): 240–267, and "Kabbalistic Traits in Borges's Narration," *Studies in Short Fiction* 8 (1971): 78–92. These two studies are reprinted in Alazraki's *Borges and the Kabbalah* (New York: Cambridge University Press, 1988), 14–37 and 38–53, respectively, along with a new essay, "Introduction," 3–13, giving his further thoughts on the parallels between Borges's work and cabala and a translation of Borges's "The Kabbalah," 54–61. Saúl Sosnowski, *Borges y la cábala: la búsqueda del verbo* (Buenos Aires: Hispamérica, 1976). Leonardo Senkman, though, has expressed concern lest parallels between Borges's work and cabala be drawn too strongly. His "La cábala y el poder de la palabra," *Nuevos Aires* [Buenos Aires] 9 (1972–73): 39–48, a polemical response to an earlier Sosnowski article on this subject, warns that Borges's aesthetic and linguistic concepts are fundamentally dissimilar to cabalistic study and practice.

5. Mary Lusky Friedman, "Origins of the Paradigm: *A Universal History of Infamy*," in her *The Emperor's Kites: A Morphology of Borges' Tales* (Durham, N.C.: Duke University Press, 1987), 55–108 (herafter cited in the text), takes an unusually detailed look at Borges's journalistic work of the 1930s. I am indebted to this exceptionally interesting chapter for much of the information presented here concerning the journalism in relation to Borges's subsequent narratives. Another very useful source of information is the compilation of Borges's journalism edited by Enrique Sacerio-Garí and Emir Rodríguez Monegal, *Textos cautivos: ensayos y reseñas en «El Hogar» (1936–1939)* (Barcelona: Tusquets Editores, 1986).

6. The editions I've used are *Historia universal de la infamia* (Buenos

Aires: Editorial Tor, 1935) and *A Universal History of Infamy*, trans. di Giovanni (New York: E. P. Dutton, 1972); hereafter cited in the text.

7. Paul de Man, "A Modern Master," in Harold Bloom, ed., *Jorge Luis Borges* (New York/New Haven/Philadelphia: Chelsea House, 1986), 21–27. This article originally appeared in the *New York Review of Books*, 19 November 1964, 8+.

8. Alazraki, "Génesis de un estilo: *Historia universal de la infamia*," *Revista Iberoamericana* 123–24 (April–September 1983): 247–61; also as "The Making of a Style: *A Universal History of Infamy*," in his *Borges and the Kabbalah*, 90–104.

9. Anthony Kerrigan's translation of this story, "The Approach to Al-Mu'tasim," is in *Ficciones* (New York: Grove Press, 1962); Norman Thomas di Giovanni's translation, "The Approach to al-Mu'tasim," is in *The Aleph and Other Stories*. Both coincide in restyling the transliteration of the Arabic name. In preparing the analyses of stories from *Ficciones* and *El Aleph*, I've used 1) *Ficciones* (Buenos Aires: Emecé, 1966); 2) *El Aleph* (Buenos Aires: Emecé, 1965); 3) *The Aleph and Other Stories*; 4) *Labyrinths: Selected Stories and Other Writings*, ed. Donald A. Yates and James E. Irby (New York: New Directions, 1962); and 5) Kerrigan's translation of *Ficciones*. All are hereafter cited in the text. In cases where varying translations appear in the English collections, I have chosen the one that best renders the quoted passage.

10. Carter Wheelock, *The Mythmaker: A Study of Motif and Symbol in the Short Stories of Jorge Luis Borges* (Austin: University of Texas Press, 1969), 152; hereafter cited in the text.

11. While the English collection *Ficciones* corresponds to the Spanish-language work of that title, there is no one English collection containing the same stories as *El Aleph*. Some of the stories of *El Aleph* appear in the 1962 miscellaneous anthology of Borges texts, *Labyrinths: Selected Short Stories and Other Writings*, while others are in the 1970 *The Aleph and Other Stories, 1933–1969, Together with Commentaries and an Autobiographical Essay*. Here the title *The Aleph* will designate the set of stories contained in *El Aleph*, while the 1970 miscellaneous anthology will be referred to as *The Aleph and Other Stories*.

12. Andrés Avellaneda chooses the H. Bustos Domecq detective stories as part of a set of Argentine texts that reflect, sometimes in covert ways and at other times unabashedly, the heightened unease and hostility between classes typical of midcentury Argentina. See his chapters "Jorge Luis Borges y Adolfo Bioy Casares. Un modelo para descifrar" and "La politización del modelo," in his *El habla de la ideología: modos de la réplica literaria en la Argentina contemporánea* (Buenos Aires: Sudamericana, 1983), 57–92.

13. Ana María Barrenechea, *La expresión de la irrealidad en la obra de Jorge Luis Borges* (Mexico: El Colegio de México, 1957); revised and expanded version, *Borges the Labyrinth Maker*, ed. and trans. Robert Lima (New York: New York University Press, 1965).

14. Stabb summarizes the critical attack on Borges in the "Against Borges" segment of his introduction to David William Foster, *Jorge Luis Borges: An Annotated Primary and Secondary Bibliography* (New York: Garland, 1984), xxxii–xxxv. Writing while the anti-Borges tendency was at its height, Rodríguez Monegal summarized and analyzed the case against the writer in the chapter "Borges entre Escila y Caribdis," in his *El juicio de los parricidas* (Buenos Aires: Deucalión, 1956), 55–79. A prime example of this negative criticism on Borges is Adolfo Prieto, *Borges y la nueva generación* (Buenos Aires: Letras Universitarias, 1954).

15. John Updike, "The Author as Librarian," *New Yorker*, 30 October 1965, 223–46.

16. John Barth, "The Literature of Exhaustion," *Atlantic*, August 1967, 29–34.

17. Michel Foucault, preface to his *Les mots et les choses* (Paris: Gallimard, 1966), 7–16; translation, *The Order of Things* (New York: Pantheon, 1970), xv–xxvi. The special interest French theorists took in Borges and his work is best represented, in English, by the critical anthology *Jorge Luis Borges*, edited by Harold Bloom (New York: Chelsea House, 1986). Emir Rodríguez Monegal was one of a number of critics who, knowing Borges's work fully and in context, expressed certain reservations about the French theorists' readings with their often-narrow, tendentious focus. He discusses both the original contribution made by these readings and their occasionally excessive zeal to find, in Borges, confirmation for tendencies of thought current on the French intellectual scene. See his "Borges y la nouvelle critique," *Revista Iberoamericana* 80 (1972): 367–90; published in English as "Borges and *la nouvelle critique*," *Diacritics* 2, no. 2 (1972): 27–34. Not only were French theorists quick to claim kinship with Borges, but Borges critics were often excited over the ready applicability of French structuralist and poststructuralist thought to the writer's stories. This enthusiasm is evident, for example, in Monique Lemaître, "Borges . . . Derrida . . . Sollers . . . Borges," *Revista Iberoamericana* 100–1 (1977): 679–82.

18. Sylvia Molloy, *Las letras de Borges* (Buenos Aires: Sudamericana, 1979). This book draws on the work of Jacques Derrida and on Molloy's experiences as one whose habits of reading have been disrupted by her encounter with Borges's texts.

19. A good example of the inquiry into Borges's exemplification of current critical preoccupations is William A. Johnson, "The Sparagmos of Myth Is the Naked Lunch of Mode: Modern Literature in the Age of Frye and Borges," *Boundary* 8, no. 2 (1980): 297–311.

20. The Spanish version takes its title from one of the pieces in the collection, "The Maker," while the 1964 English translation, *Dreamtigers*, uses the English neologism Borges coined for a different text. Despite the divergent titles, *El hacedor* and *Dreamtigers* contain the same material.

21. The editions I've used in preparing these analyses are *El informe de*

Brodie (Buenos Aires: Emecé, 1971) and *Doctor Brodie's Report*, trans. Norman Thomas di Giovanni (New York: Bantam Books, 1973); hereafter cited in the text.

22. *Elogio de la sombra* (Buenos Aires: Emecé, 1969) and *In Praise of Darkness*, trans. Norman Thomas di Giovanni (New York: E. P. Dutton, 1974), are the editions I've consulted.

23. "Harto de los laberintos," interview with César Fernández Moreno, *Mundo Nuevo* [Paris] 18 (December 1967): 8–29. This famous interview also appeared as "Weary of Labyrinths," *Encounter* 32, no. 4 (1969): 3–14.

24. The editions I've used are *El libro de arena* (Barcelona: Plaza y Janés, 1977) and *The Book of Sand*, trans. Norman Thomas di Giovanni (New York: E. P. Dutton, 1977).

Part 2

THE WRITER

Introduction

Borges was at his best with a conversation partner well versed in his work and knowledgeable about literature in general. With Fernando Sorrentino, a talented short story writer and critical editor, Borges pursues a zigzag route through some of his favored topics. He discusses his two most famous preferences: for the short story over the novel, and for frank stylization over the attempt to make art resemble life. In looking back over his career, Borges does not miss the opportunity to give a slightly mocking portrait of himself as an excitable young avant-garde poet. His derisive remarks on his 1935 *A Universal History of Infamy* call attention to his long, gradual transition from the essay toward short fiction; he alludes also to his belief that a phobia of authoring short stories was what delayed his emergence as a practitioner of this form. Sorrentino speaks for many Borges fans when he expresses disappointment at the relative simplicity of language and construction that sets the author's late fiction apart from the stories of his high period; Borges, while seeming to agree that the plainer tales carry less force, really defends the shift in his concept and practice of the short story. Sorrentino draws Borges out on several other themes, among them the detective stories of G. K. Chesterton and Arthur Conan Doyle; the Germanic languages, both modern and ancient; the short fiction of Kafka; *Don Quixote*; and Buenos Aires as it was during the author's childhood. Borges, who was extremely fond of literary games, refers to one of his favorites: trying to imagine literary history or masterworks as being somehow other than, in fact, they are.

Interview, 1973

Fernando Sorrentino: When and where was Jorge Luis Borges born?

Jorge Luis Borges: I was born on August 24, 1899. I'm very happy about this because I like the nineteenth century very much, although it could be said to the detriment of the nineteenth century that it led to the twentieth century, which I find less admirable. I was born on Tucumán Street between Esmeralda and Suipacha, and I know that all the houses on the block were one-storey affairs except for the combination grocery-saloon, which had a second storey, and every house was constructed in the style of the Argentine Society of Writers, except that the house in which I was born was much more modest. That is, it had two windows with iron grillwork, the door to the street with its ring-shaped knocker, then the vestibule, next the inner door, then the rooms, the side courtyard, and the well. And in the bottom of the well—I found this out much later—there was a turtle for purifying the water. So my grandparents, my parents, and I had drunk turtle water for years and it hadn't done us any harm; nowadays it would disgust us to think we're drinking turtle water. My mother remembers having heard as a little girl—besides the bullets of the 1890 Revolution—one exceptional bullet: my grandfather went out and said General Ricardo López Jordán had been assassinated right around the corner. Some people say the assassin, under contract with the Urquiza family, provoked and then killed him. I believe this is false. Actually, López Jordán had had this man's father killed, so this fellow picked a quarrel with López Jordán, killed him with one shot, fled down Tucumán Street and was captured after he had made it to Florida Street.

From Fernando Sorrentino, *Seven Conversations with Jorge Luis Borges*, trans. Clark M. Zlotchew (Troy, N.Y.: Whitston Publishing Co., 1982), 1–4, 22–24, 33, 37–39, 85–88, 121–26, 137–39, 145–46. Originally published as *Siete conversaciones con Jorge Luis Borges* (Buenos Aires: Casa Pardo, 1973). Reprinted by permission of Fernando Sorrentino and Clark M. Zlotchew.

FS: At that time, where did the built-up portion of the City end?

JLB: I can give you two answers. Formerly, the City ended at Centro América Street—that is, [today's] Pueyrredón. Mother remembers this. But my mother is ninety-five years old. Beyond that point there were vacant lots, country homes, brick kilns, a large lagoon, clusters of shacks, people riding on horseback, inhabitants of the outlying slums. But when I was a child we moved to the outlying Palermo district, which was at one end of the City, and at that time the buildings ended precisely at the Pacífico Bridge, on Maldonado Creek, where the Paloma Café still stands, I believe.

FS: Used to stand: there's a pizzeria there now.

JLB: Everything is going to the dogs! They used to have *truco* [a card game] competitions there. And then there were no more buildings up to the Belgrano district, let's say somewhere around Federico Lacroze Street, I suppose. But in all that space there were a great many vacant lots. Maldonado Creek apparently gave rise to bad neighborhoods no matter where—the Palermo district, or Villa Crespo, or Flores—neighborhoods of prostitution, of hoodlums.

FS: Is that where your "Hombre de la esquina rosada" takes place?

JLB: Yes, but a little further out. I had it take place beyond Flores and gave it an indeterminate date. I did it deliberately. I believe that a writer should never attempt a contemporary theme nor a very precise topography. Otherwise people are immediately going to find mistakes. Or if they don't find them, they're going to look for them, and if they look for them, they'll find them. That's why I prefer to have my stories take place in somewhat indeterminate places and many years ago. For example, the best story I've ever written, "La intrusa," takes place in Turdera, on the outskirts of Adrogué or of Lomas; it takes place more or less at the end of the last century or at the beginning of this one. And I did it deliberately so no one could say to me: "No, people aren't like that." The other day I came upon a young fellow who told me he was going to write a novel about a café called "El Socorrito," at the corner of Juncal and Esmeralda: a contemporary novel. I told him not to say the café was "El Socorrito" and not to say the time is the present, because if he did someone was going to tell him: "The people in that café don't talk that way" or "The atmosphere is phony." So I think a certain distance in time and space is appropriate. Besides, I believe that the idea that literature should treat contemporary themes is relatively new. If I'm not mistaken, the *Iliad* was probably written two or three centuries after the fall of Troy. I think that freedom of imagination demands that we search for subjects which are distant in time and space, or if not, on other planets, the way those who write science-fiction are doing right now. Otherwise, we are somewhat tied down by reality, and literature already seems too much like journalism.

FS: Do you mean you don't believe in psychological literature somehow?

JLB: Yes, of course I believe in psychological literature, and I think that all literature is fundamentally psychological. The acts performed by a character are facets of or ways of describing that character. Juan Ramón Jiménez said he could imagine a *Don Quixote* with adventures other than those contained in the book. I believe that what is important in *Don Quixote* are the characters possessed by Alonso Quijano and Sancho [Panza]. But we can imagine other fictional events. Cervantes was aware of that fact when he wrote the second part, which I think is far superior to the first. What doesn't seem right to me is for literature to become confused with journalism or with history. It appears to me that literature should be psychological and should be imaginative. I, at least when I'm alone, tend to think and to imagine. But I wouldn't be able to tell you—of course my being practically blind enters into it—the number of chairs there are in this room. And maybe you could do it now only if you were to count them . . . .

FS: I understand that in your readings you've had one favorite author after another since you were young.

JLB: Yes, but I believe they're the same ones. It's just that I thought it was more honorable to name others. But I think they were Wells and Stevenson and Kipling from the first. . . .

FS: And no Spaniards?

JLB: Spaniards? Well . . . *Don Quixote*, yes. And Fray Luis de León too. Spanish literature began admirably; the Spanish *romances* are beautiful. But what happened afterward? I think the decadence of Spanish literature ran parallel with the decadence of the Spanish Empire: from the time the "Invincible" Armada was destroyed, from the time Spain failed to understand Protestantism, from the time Spain remained more distant from France than we in Latin America did, from the time Spanish-American Modernism was being forged in the shadow of Hugo and Verlaine while in Spain they were unaware of this.

FS: According to what you've just said, would Quevedo and Góngora fall within the early stages of Spanish decadence?

JLB: They already had a kind of rigidity, of stiffness in them which one doesn't find, for example, in Fray Luis de León. When you read Fray Luis, you realize that he was a better person than Quevedo or than Góngora, who were vain, baroque people who wanted to dazzle the reader. And they were a little younger, compared with Fray Luis. But look at the "Coplas" of Manrique, for example. Truly a great poem! And it wasn't written for the purpose of dazzling anyone. Why do I consider Fray Luis de León a better poet than Quevedo? Not line for line; Quevedo, no doubt, is more inventive verbally. But at the same time, one feels that Fray Luis de León was a better person than Quevedo. Quevedo, if he had lived at the present time, what would he have been? He would have been a follower of Franco, of course. He would have been a Nationalist. In Buenos Aires he would have been a Peronist. He was a man who didn't understand anything of what was taking place in his own time. For instance, he was unaware of the Protestant movement, which was important. They weren't even aware of the discovery of America. They were all more interested in the disastrous wars and defeats they were suffering in Flanders than in the New World. And Montesquieu realized this. He said: "The Indies [i.e., America] are the main thing; Spain is secondary; *L'Espagne n'est que accessoire.*" And there was no Spaniard who understood that, not even Cervantes, I believe. Cervantes was more interested in the wars in Flanders, which, of course, were disastrous, because [the Spaniards] were beaten by people who weren't even soldiers.

FS: What do you think of medieval Spanish literature? The *Poema del Cid* or the Archpriest of Hita, for example?

JLB: I think the Cid is a dull and unimaginative poem. Think of the heroic spirit there is in the [French] *Chanson de Roland*, centuries earlier. Think of Anglo-Saxon epic poetry and of Scandinavian poetry. The Cid actually is a very slow poem, very clumsily done.

FS: And the Archpriest of Hita?

JLB: I don't think he's a very important author. Now, Saint John of the Cross was; he was a great poet, of course. And Garcilaso, too. But what was Garcilaso? He was an Italian poet gone astray in Spain. This is so true that his contemporaries didn't understand him. Castillejo, for example, never came to have a feel—as Lugones remembers and Jaimes Freyre remembered too—for the music of the hendeca-syllable. They were accustomed to the octosyllable, just like our gaucho troubadors. And then there's Spain's eighteenth century: it's impov-erished to the utmost. The nineteenth century is a disgrace! Spain has no novelist like the Portuguese Eça de Queiroz, for example. And at present all the important poets that Spain has produced are the products of Modernism, and Modernism came to them from Spanish-America. And Spanish-language prose has been renovated by Groussac and by Reyes [writing in the Americas]. . . .

Now, as for the fact that I've lost my sight, the process has been so gradual that it was never a sudden blow. I mean to say, the world has been becoming more and more blurred for me; books have lost their letters, my friends have lost their faces, but all that has been happening over a period of many years. Besides, I knew that would be my fate because my father, my grandmother, that is, my grandparents, and, I think, my great-great-grandfather, were blind when they died. My vision was never good. Proof of that is that if I think about my childhood I don't think of the neighborhood, I don't think about my parents' faces. What I think about are minuscule things, seen close up. For example, I think I remember more or less the illustrations in encyclo-pedias, in travel books, in *The Thousand and One Nights*, in dictionaries. I think I remember quite precisely the stamps in a large album there was at home, and all that because they were the only things I saw well, which is typical of the minute vision of the nearsighted.

FS: Since you've referred to that period of your childhood, I'd like to ask you if you took part in the usual leisure activities of the time, and if so, what they were. I don't know . . . maybe soccer?

JLB: Soccer, at that time, was relegated to one or two English schools, but I suppose most people probably hadn't heard of it or weren't interested in it. At any rate, it was probably thought of as the sport of some rich kids in the schools of Lomas or Belgrano. And I think it's strange—coincidentally, I was talking about this last night —it's strange that England—which I love so much—provokes so much hatred in the world but that nevertheless one argument that could be used is never used against England: that of having filled the world with stupid sports. It's strange that people who don't like England don't confront her with having filled the world with cricket, with golf—

although golf is Scottish—with soccer. I think that is one of the sins which could be imputed to England. . . .

FS: What role do the works of Shakespeare play in your life?

JLB: They play an important role, but outside of *Macbeth* and *Hamlet*, they pertain to verbal memories rather than to memories of situations or of characters. For example, what I've re-read most in Shakespeare are the sonnets. I could quote so many lines for you. . . . Just as I could quote so many lines from his dramatic works too. . . . I think of Shakespeare above all as a craftsman of words. For example, I see him closer to Joyce than to the great novelists, where character is the most important thing. That's the reason I'm skeptical about translations of Shakespeare, because . . . what is most essential and most precious in him is the verbal aspect. I wonder to what extent the verbal can be translated. A short time ago someone told me: "It's impossible to translate Shakespeare into Spanish." And I answered him: "As impossible as it is to translate him into English." Because if we were to translate Shakespeare into an English which is not the English of Shakespeare, a great deal would be lost. There are even sentences of Shakespeare's that only exist if pronounced with those same words, in that same order and with that same melody.

FS: But what you've said is, in a way, a slur against Shakespeare, if we remember that you once praised those books which, like *Don Quixote*, can come away from the worst translations unscathed.

JLB: Yes, the truth is that I'm contradicting myself here. Because, by the way, I remember that we saw, together with Letizia Alvarez de Toledo, a production of *Macbeth* in Spanish, performed by terrible actors, with terrible stage sets, using an abominable translation, and yet we left the theater very, very thrilled. So I believe I made a slip when I said what I said before. And I don't mind your recording my retraction, because I don't think of myself as infallible, not at all, not even when it comes to my own work.

FS: Readers usually believe, unjustly perhaps, that they can demand a particular type of behavior from a writer they admire. I, who have been dazzled by the stories in *Ficciones* and in *El Aleph*, take the liberty of criticizing you for having given up, in the stories of *El informe de Brodie*, those complex plots. How would you answer me?

JLB: My answer to you is that I've done it deliberately, because since I've been told there are other people who are writing that type of literature, and no doubt they're doing it better than I, I've attempted something different. But it's possible that this is my conscious motive and, for that very reason, not too important. Instead, I believe there is something that has led me to write stories of another type: being tired of mirrors, of labyrinths, of people who are other people, of games with time. Why not suppose that being tired of all that, I want to write stories somewhat the way others do?

FS: Of course, I understand that. But, speaking for myself, I wouldn't think of reading *El informe de Brodie* again, yet I read and re-read *El Aleph* (I know it almost by heart).

JLB: That might be due to the fact that when I wrote *El Aleph*, the writing was carried out in a kind of literary plenitude. On the other hand, it could be that I'm now in a state of decline and my current works could reflect a sort of decadence in me. It would be perfectly natural because it's biologically understandable. In August [1971] I'll be seventy-two years old, and it's only logical for what I'm writing now to be inferior to what I wrote earlier. I think this biological explanation is a pretty likely one. But, at the same time, since I'm in the habit of writing, I keep doing what I can. Now, I don't know if you've read a story of mine called "El congreso," because I got the idea for that story more than thirty years ago but wrote it a short time ago. There might possibly be some disparity in the plot, which of course is a fantastic plot—not fantastic in the supernatural sense but rather in the sense of impossible—because it has to do with a mystical experience I haven't had. My aim was to narrate something in which I didn't fully believe to see how it would turn out. . . .

FS: Aside from Spanish and English, which were your native tongues, what other languages are you able to read?

JLB: When I had my sight, I was able to read German and could enjoy German literature. A few days ago we spoke of Germany; I would venture to say Germany has produced, among so many other things, something I think is superior to everything else it has given us, even thinking of some admirable poets, even thinking of Heine, or of Angelus Silesius, or maybe Hölderlin, and that something is the German language, which I think is extraordinarily beautiful, which I think is made for poetry.

FS: I seemed to notice in your translation of Kafka's The *Metamorphosis*, that you differ from your usual style. . . .

JLB: Well, that's due to the fact that I'm not the author of the translation of that text. A proof of this—in addition to my word—is that I know something about German; I know the work is entitled *Die Verwandlung* and not *Die Metamorphose*, and I know it should have been translated as *The Transformation*. But, since the French translator preferred—perhaps as a salute from afar to Ovid—*La Métamorphose*, we subserviently did the same thing here. That translation has to be —I have that impression because of a few turns of phrase—the work of some Spaniard. What I did translate were the other stories by Kafka which are in the same volume published by Editorial Losada. But, to simplify matters—maybe for merely typographical reasons, they preferred to attribute the translation of the entire volume to me, and used a perhaps anonymous translation floating around out there. . . .

FS: Coming back to the subject of languages, from which we've strayed, what memories do you have of your experiences as a Latinist?

JLB: Memories that are clearer than my memory of the language itself, of Latin. It saddens me to think I devoted six or seven years to the study of Latin, that I came to enjoy Virgil's poetry and the prose of Tacitus and Seneca, and that now all that I have left of all that Latin are a few Latin phrases. But—and I don't know if I've already mentioned this—I think having forgotten Latin is in itself a kind of possession since Latin teaches us a kind of economy, a kind of strictness, a love for the sententious. And I believe this is beneficial in the handling of other languages. And at this point I recall a line of Robert Browning. It goes:

> Latin, the language of marble.

I think this refers not only to the fact that Latin inscriptions are common, but to the fact that the Latin language seems made to be carved in marble. It's as if there were a natural affinity between those two languages, between Latin and marble.

FS: And it never occurred to you to study Greek?

JLB: No. For one thing, there's a reason I usually give when I'm asked why I don't know Greek; it's that there are so many people who already know it for me. But I don't know if that's the real reason. The truth is that I've felt attracted—just a moment ago I spoke of my admiration for German, and everyone knows how much I admire English—I've felt attracted instead to the Germanic languages. At

123

present, after nine years of having devoted myself to Old English, I'm studying Old Icelandic, a language related to Anglo-Saxon. Besides, I'm about to become seventy-two years old and am not able to undertake the study of languages whose roots are different from those of the languages I already know. For example, I would have liked to know Hebrew, but I know it's beyond my present capabilities. When I was a young man, I would have been able to do it. I know that essentially the same thing is happening to me with Old English and with Old Icelandic. I know I won't ever possess them, but I also know that this sort of slow voyage toward the impossible somehow is a pleasure. And I think I said all this in one of the poems of my book, *Elogio de la sombra*.

FS: Haven't you ever felt a kind of remorse when reading the Greek classics in translation?

JLB: No. I used to think about this the same way I thought about Arabic. Not knowing Greek and Arabic allowed me to read, so to speak, the *Odyssey* and *A Thousand and One Nights* in many different versions, so that this poverty also brought me a kind of richness. . . .

FS: Then it was difficult for you to come to your present linguistic conventions.

JLB: Yes. The truth is that to reach the point of writing in a more or less uncluttered manner, a more or less decorous manner, I've had to reach the age of seventy. Because there was a time when I wanted to write in Old Spanish; later I tried to write in the manner of those seventeenth-century authors who, in turn, were trying to write like Seneca—a Latinized Spanish. And then it occurred to me that it was my duty to be Argentinean. So I acquired a dictionary of Argentinisms and devoted myself to being a professional died-in-the-wool Argentinean to such an extent that my mother told me that she didn't understand what I had written because she wasn't familiar with that dictionary and because she spoke like a normal Argentinean. And now I believe I've come to write in a more or less straightforward manner. I remember something George Moore said that impressed me. Wishing to praise someone, he said: "He wrote in an almost anonymous style." And I thought that was the greatest compliment an author could be given: "He wrote in an almost anonymous style."

FS: Then it's obvious that between the *Historia universal de la infamia* and . . .

JLB: Well, the *Historia universal de la infamia* is written in a baroque style, but it was done as a kind of joke, you see? A not very amusing joke . . . but, in short, I couldn't think of anything else to write.

FS: Of course. Personally, I enjoy reading *El Aleph* but not the *Historia universal de la infamia.*

JLB: Oh, yes; of course, there's a major difference. The *Historia universal de la infamia* was written by a beginner and *El Aleph* was written by a man with some literary experience and who was mature enough to stop playing certain games, and to stop indulging in certain kinds of mischief or pranks.

FS: How did you feel when you saw *Fervor de Buenos Aires*, your first book, on the market?

JLB: The expression "on the market" is exaggerated because I didn't stock the bookstores with it; I didn't think anyone could be interested in what I was writing. But I recall that I was very excited when I held a copy in my hands. Why that was so is a mystery to me, because after all, there isn't much difference between a manuscript and a book in print, and even less between a typewritten copy and a book in print—although what I actually handed in was a manuscript. Nevertheless, that difference does exist. Because that was my first book, and things make a deep impression when they occur for the first time. As for prizes, people have been very generous with me; I've won important literary prizes, and none has impressed me as much as that Second Municipal Prize for Literature in Prose I was awarded in 1928, because it was the first prize I ever won.

FS: Did you ever receive any literary advice, in your youth, that turned out to be especially useful for you?

JLB: Yes. My father gave me that advice. He told me to write a lot, to discard a lot, and not to rush into print, so that the first book I had published, *Fervor de Buenos Aires*, was really my third book. My father told me that when I had written a book I judged to be not altogether unworthy of publication, he would pay for the printing of the book, but that it was each man for himself and I shouldn't ask anyone for advice. Besides, I was too timid to show anyone what I was writing, so that when the book appeared, my family and friends read it for the first time. I hadn't shown it to anyone and it wouldn't have occurred to me to ask for a prologue either. . . .

FS: Did you like the detective novels of [Sir Arthur] Conan Doyle?

Part 2

JLB: The truth is, I liked them very much and I think I still do. And I think one could say of Conan Doyle's novels the same thing that could be said of Estanislao del Campo's *Fausto*: more important than the plot—or, in the case of *Fausto*, the parody of the tragedy, let's say, of Dr. Faust or of the opera based on Goethe's work—is the friendship between the two characters. And in the case of *The Sign of the Four*, of *A Study in Scarlet*, of *The Hound of the Baskervilles*, of the *Memoirs of Sherlock Holmes*, of the *Adventures of Sherlock Holmes*, I think that more important than the plots—which are customarily very poor, outside of that of *The Red-Headed League*—is the friendship that exists between Sherlock Holmes and Watson: the fact that friendship is possible between a very intelligent man and a man who is rather a fool; the fact that they are friends nevertheless, and think highly of and understand one another. I think the atmosphere in Conan Doyle's novels (that house on Baker Street, those two gentlemen bachelors who live alone, the arrival of someone with the news of a crime, all that) is more important than the detective plot. Because, naturally, there are authors who are infinitely inferior to Conan Doyle—Van Dine, for example—who have thought up much more ingenious plots and nonetheless are still mediocre. Maybe Conan Doyle understood that his readers were satisfied with the friendship between Watson and Sherlock Holmes.

FS: And I, with all modesty, would add another of Conan Doyle's virtues: his sense of humor.

JLB: I believe so. But Chesterton exaggerated when he said Conan Doyle wrote predominantly for humorous effect. I don't believe that; I believe that while he was writing, he believed in his detective. What's more, I think this has been beneficial for him. If he had planned on making—as Chesterton said—a ridiculous figure of Sherlock Holmes, he would have failed. And the fact is, in any event, the public hasn't taken him that way. On the contrary, when I was a boy and read those novels and then when I read them again throughout my life, I always thought of Sherlock Holmes as an admirable character and not, in spite of a certain vanity or a certain pretentiousness, as a ridiculous character. I don't think that was the author's intent and I don't think Sherlock Holmes has been taken as a ridiculous character by the readers. He has been looked upon as a loveable character, and Watson too, and above all, the friendship between the two of them.

FS: This question is more to satisfy my own curiosity than that of the readers: I'd like to know if you, as a child, read a novel of Conan Doyle's which I liked very much: *The Lost World*.

JLB: Yes, at the time I thought it was very good. I recall that plateau in the middle of Brazil. . . . It came out in installments in *Sun Magazine*, and I remember the illustrations: there was Professor Challenger . . . and the other characters, whose names I don't remember. And it was in *Sun Magazine* too that I read *The Hound of the Baskervilles*. All those novels were published in installments. I remember having read, in a biography of Oscar Wilde, that a Mr. Lippincott, I believe, was going to start a review entitled *Lippincott's Magazine*. So, he invited two writers to luncheon and proposed that they write installment novels for his magazine. And out of that luncheon came Oscar Wilde's *The Picture of Dorian Gray* and, I believe, Conan Doyle's *The Sign of the Four*. In addition, Wilde and Conan Doyle were friends and furthermore they were both Irish, although Conan Doyle was born in Edinburgh, in Scotland. It seemed strange to me that he was considered Irish but, irrefutably, I was told: "If a cat were to give birth in an oven, would you call what she gave birth to kittens or bread?" And I think they were right, don't you? . . .

FS: A little while ago you told me the novel was a genre which would finally disappear. Have you felt this way for a long time or did you ever, in your youth, think of writing a novel?

JLB: No, I never thought of writing novels. I think if I began to write a novel, I would realize that it's nonsensical and that I wouldn't follow through on it. Possibly this is an excuse dreamed up by my laziness. But I think Conrad and Kipling have demonstrated that a short story—not too short, what we could call, using the English term, a "long short story"—is able to contain everything a novel contains, with less strain on the reader. In the case of what, for me, is one of the greatest novels in the world, *Don Quixote*, I think the reader would be able to do very well without the first part and could rely on the second, because he wouldn't lose anything, since he would find it all in the second part. Juan Ramón Jiménez said he could imagine a Don Quixote that would be essentially the same, but in which the episodes would be different, since the episodes are nothing more than vehicles for revealing to us the character of the protagonist, or perhaps of the two protagonists.

FS: What advantage do you see in the short story over the novel?

JLB: The essential advantage I see in it is that the short story can be taken in at a single glance. On the other hand, in the novel the consecutive is more noticeable. And then there's the fact that a work of three hundred pages depends on padding, on pages which are mere nexuses between one part and another. On the other hand, it's possible for everything to be essential, or more or less essential, or—shall we say—appear to be essential in a short story. I think there are stories of Kipling's that are as dense as a novel, or of Conrad's too. It's true they're not too short.

Part 3

THE CRITICS

Introduction

Because of Carter Wheelock's long-standing critical involvement with the complexities of Borges's famous baroque stories, it is especially worth noting how he has adapted to the plainer tales of the author's late period. In "Borges and the 'Death' of the Text," he treats some of these stories as one would parables—that is, proceeding on the assumption that their spare surface both hides and points to a wealth of meanings. Here Wheelock proposes allegorical interpretations for several narratives, with reading and writing as the disguised themes. Reading Borges with the relativism that pervades this author's writing, Wheelock makes it clear that he is speculating about, rather than defining, the significance to be found in these stories.

David William Foster's "Borges and Structuralism: Toward an Implied Poetics" helps account for a seeming anomaly: this author, who produced his major work before the rise of French structuralism and who remained impervious to this intellectual tendency, was embraced by the structuralists as one of their own. Foster examines several of Borges's most famous stories for what they imply about certain issues central to structuralist thought, such as the relativism of truths and the constructed or patterned nature of knowledge. The article emphasizes the need to keep in mind that, while Borges's stories are based on concepts and propositions, these have a status unlike that of the ideas expounded in philosophical work or literary commentary. The notions underlying the short fiction may be very similar to those found in basic texts of structuralism, but they are manifested with the aesthetically pleasing unpredictability, ambiguity, and memorability of art.

Carter Wheelock

In an unpublished lecture given at the University of Texas (Austin) in 1980, Jean Franco alluded to "the reader-writer relationship implied in some of the stories" of Jorge Luis Borges' *El informe de Brodie* (1970). Since her remark was made in relation to textual interpretation and not to the implications of style, it can be understood to mean that in the stories in question (which were not specified) there is an insinuated artistic statement about readers and writers. I have seen no critical development of this idea, which I take here as my subject. In the *Brodie* volume there are implications that the relationship between the author and the reader of fiction requires their cooperation in the "murder" of the text. I use this metaphorical term because I hope to show that Borges resorts to plots culminating in murder, crucifixion, execution, and other kinds of betrayal or abandonment to suggest the act of going beyond the literal values of a text to reach its aesthetic effect or supra-intellectual "meaning."

My thesis is that Borges, noted for writing fiction about the nature of fiction, has at times played on the idea that when a reader has finished the text he must let go of it; he must abandon the notion that the intention of a body of language is to present a subject or to impart any kind of objective reality beyond the presence and function of the text as a creative process. For that purpose the subject-matter is indifferent. The reader cannot advance to the plane of aesthetic value so long as he clings to the intellectual content of the language. Climbing a ladder, so to speak, he must finally scorn the base means of ascent in order to meet the writer on the level of wordless understanding.

In order to deal with illustrative texts from *Brodie* I must first lay a theoretical framework. Throughout his career Borges has clung to some of his earliest ideas, and in *Brodie* we can discern the application of notions which he expressed in an essay published in 1932, "El arte narrativo y la magia" (*Discusión*). He speaks there of psychological

From "Borges and the 'Death' of the Text," *Hispanic Review* 53 (1985):151–61. Reprinted by permission.

realism, in which every event must be made believable according to criteria which simulate objective reality. He contrasts this with un-realism, in which the literary credibility of a character or occurrence is established in the text itself by subtle prefiguration. That is, something which the reader would otherwise reject as unworthy of literary faith is quite acceptable if it has been "prophesied" by previous suggestive details. The effect of the prior insinuations is to supply the reader with attributes of the thing to come, so that when it does come it requires no convincing description. The reader supplies the image of it himself, out of accumulated suggestions, and because he supplies it he "be-lieves" it. What Borges is saying is that the reader of fiction is not looking for a text's agreement with reality but for completeness of idea, the fullness and coherence of his own mental furniture. The new and the unusual are easily scorned and rejected if they hit the reader cold, but they are accepted—recognized as somehow legitimately "in place"—if they are already half-born in the reader's awareness. In his own practice in fiction, Borges shows that the prophesying details do not have to be overt images or statements; they are generally subtle hints out of which the reader finally abstracts what is never openly presented.

In the same essay Borges refers to this narrational trick as "magical causality" and compares it with prefiguration of a kind visible in prim-itive or mythic thought. Any perceived or imagined relationship be-tween two objects or events—simultaneity, sequence, similarity, spatial closeness—is taken by the primitive thinker as an identity, a cause-and-effect connection, or an explanation. Among his examples Borges offers the case of a primitive man who cuts himself to make the blood flow, expecting the imitative skies to make it rain. In other words, literary "prophesying" works on the principle of mental asso-ciation or cognitive correspondence, and it matters little how objectively justified the association may be. Whether it rains or not, the self-cutting primitive thinker integrates and satisfies his *mind* with that action, and mental satisfaction is all he really intends. His failure to bring rain does not destroy his belief in self-cutting, because it has a ceremonial value although he does not understand it as mere ceremony. In Borges' view, the reading of literature is the same kind of mind-satisfying ritual, and its value increases in proportion to the reader's realization of its purely ceremonial character—his awareness that contact with objective reality is not the purpose of the text. Aesthetic thrill, which for Borges is the only true value or "meaning" of literature, lies precisely in the reader's awareness that "art," the process of mental creation, has occurred, and this realization happens when the thing created is seen to be a pure figment having no status in nature, particularly when it comes as an intuition without conceptual form. Borges has famously characterized the aesthetic happening as "the imminence of a revelation that never comes" ("La muralla y los libros," *Otras inquisiciones* [1952]). Aesthesia lies in the self-awareness of the creative thought-process when it has no intellective product to eclipse it.

Borges never says all of what he means. His art has been well described as one of allusion, and even when reading his essays we must understand him by extension. In fiction, I want to show, he brings about a much more subtle "prophecy" than his essay describes. This, too, must be explained briefly before turning to the literature. Wellek and Warren (*Theory of Literature* [New York, 1961], p. 182) have seen "the meaning and function of literature as centrally present in metaphor and myth." Metaphor is perhaps the simplest form of literary unreality (of pure art) and exemplifies the elementary transcendence of the literal content of language. If a brave man is called a lion, the reality highlighted is courage. Courage is not named but is understood, and the objective content—man and lion—can be taken away; they are only the "ladder," not the meaning. When a more sophisticated text, besides speaking of man and lion, gives allusive details suggesting analogous comparisons—alternative metaphors for courage that are not actually named—the effect is to make us realize that even the abstraction "courage" is not the final meaning. The alternatives draw our attention to the very process by which we abstract a reality without naming it. Thus we transcend not only man and lion but also the intellectual product, courage, and have an intuition or conception of the metaphorical procedure, which is a function of mind, not of external reality. We have transcended a reality without abstracting another of an objective kind; thought is aware only of itself as it stands in expectation of what it knows will not materialize, in the "imminence of a revelation."

The first thing I want to show is not that Borges achieves aesthetic effect (this would be impossible, since it is only a personal experience) but that he provides the elements of the process and at the same time alludes to its operation through plots and details which comprise parables or allegories. In "El evangelio según Marcos" (*Brodie*) the young medical student Espinosa is 33 years old, is noted for oratory and kindness, has healing powers, and has a name suggesting thorns; in short, he has attributes of Christ. Christ has not been mentioned, but these attributes have prepared the reader not to reject an incredible event, Espinosa's crucifixion. Without them his execution would be utterly baffling because there is no apparent reason for it; with them it remains strange and surprising but is vaguely appropriate, and the reader is driven to find a basis in logic if he cannot simply accept that mysteriously fitting occurrence. Even without an explanation there is a symmetry of completeness in the crucifixion of a protagonist who has been equated by insinuation with Jesus. But if we can abstract courage from the equation of a man with a lion, there must be something to be abstracted from Espinosa's identification with Christ. To help us, Borges provides a second metaphor, an alternative comparison. Espinosa is isolated in a ranch house with a family of illiterates named Gutre. To entertain them he reads from the Gospel of Mark, which he appreciates for its aesthetic value but does not literally believe. During repeated readings over several days the slow-witted Gutres give rapt attention to the words and follow Espinosa around the house with adulation. The Gutre daughter comes to his bed uninvited and gives herself to him without speaking, embracing him, or kissing him. After asking Espinosa to confirm their literal conception of hell as a fiery punishment, and to verify their inference that even those who crucified Christ were saved by that action, the Gutres curse him, spit on him, and push him to a shed where they have built a cross.

The second metaphor is the equation of Christ, and of Espinosa, with a literary text. Christ is the incarnate Word, the living embodiment of a corpus of language also called the Word of God. Espinosa, by reading to illiterates, becomes their oral text. The Christ-text was predestined by God the author to be sacrificed by and for man the reader. The Gospel as language, we can infer, is predestined to be sacrificed in the letter for the sake of its transcending "spirit"; the text itself comments on how it is to be read, for Espinosa as the Gutres' oral text does not believe literally in the words he is transmitting, taking them only as conveyors of inexpressible experience. How do the Gutres read? At first with close attention and mental devotion, seeing the text but not through it. The Gutre girl accepts it passively, without conversation, embrace, or kiss. In the end the readers comprehend that if the text is sacrificed in the letter, it will transcend itself.

In February, 1982, conversing with Borges about the *Brodie* stories, I mentioned that "El evangelio" can be read as a tale about the crucifixion of a literary text. Borges said, "Yes, you are right. If I could write that story again, I would make it clearer that Espinosa wanted to be crucified." That a piece of literature should want to be negated in its literal significance in order to be art, not reality, testifies to Borges' intention that his reader will take his fiction for its aesthetic value, not its ideas. Even the interpretation given above—that the story is about how a text should be read—is "negated" or superseded by the aesthetic thrill available to the reader prior to intellectual paraphrase. Interpretations are irrelevant to aesthetic enjoyment.

A writer cannot be certain that his literature will have aesthetic value for the reader. This idea, the uncertainty of success, has also been turned into a story, I suggest, in "El otro duelo" (*Brodie*). In this one, execution metaphorizes the writer's action. Borges says this story is a true happening in Argentine history. There are two gauchos, Silveira and Cardoso, who have made their reputations as fighters with the knife. Although they are rivals for fame and bitter enemies, they have never fought each other because their mutual hatred is the only thing that gives meaning to their "poor and monotonous lives." They go into the army, both are captured by the enemy, and both are destined for execution along with other prisoners. Knowing of their rivalry, the enemy commander prepares a special death for them. They are stood side by side, their throats are cut simultaneously, and they run a race. Each runs a short way and falls. Cardoso falls with his arms outstretched, and it is hinted that because of that gesture he wins the race; but, we are told, perhaps he never knew it. I trust the analogy is clear. When a writer predestines his text to "death," undermining its credibility as denotative language or realism, he cuts its throat but makes it run its course nonetheless. Dying, it stretches out its arms, not knowing whether it has reached its aesthetic goal. This should remind us of the Prologue to *Artificios* (1944), now a part of *Ficciones*, in which Borges wrote that in "La secta del Fénix" he undertook to evoke by degrees—that is, by prefiguration—a common phenomenon which, never named, would turn out to be unequivocal, adding that he did not know how successful he had been. He later admitted to insistent critics that the common phenomenon was the sex act. But the story's prophesying details are numerous, varied, and suggestive of other things, of which the sex act is representative by analogy—such as the reading of a literary text to its climactic or aesthetic moment.

I believe I have made my point sufficiently clear concerning prefiguration and the inclusion of "second metaphors." In discussing the stories to follow, I will concentrate primarily on the central analogy, textual "murder."

The most gripping story of *El informe de Brodie* is "La intrusa." The Nilsen brothers, Cristián and Eduardo, are Godless and immoral, devoted only to each other. The older, Cristián, brings home a silent, servile girl named Juliana, and after a while he offers to share her sexual favors with Eduardo, who readily accepts. Eduardo becomes too fond of the girl, and she seems to prefer him because although he accepted the arrangement he had not proposed it. Jealousy grows in Eduardo to the point of threatening the fraternal relationship. The girl, at first a link between the men, has become almost a barrier. With Cristián taking the initiative, the brothers sell her to a whorehouse; but when Cristián finds Eduardo going to see her on the sly, she is brought back home. The jealousy remains, so Cristián kills her, and when Eduardo learns of it the two men embrace over her body.

Like others, this story suggests immediate parallels. It brings to mind, through inconspicuous details, the reconciliation of God and man wrought through the sacrifice of Christ (Juliana possesses a Crucifix and is "the servant of all," so to speak). Cain is mentioned, and the story can be taken as the Cain and Abel episode with God omitted—that is, with God dwelling in both men and not up in the sky, so that a worshipful sacrifice has to be mutual. But again, the details prophesy more than the obvious. Cristián the writer offers his text, Juliana, to Eduardo the reader. The text seems to prefer the reader because it is the writer's gift; the reader has not "proposed" it. The reader becomes too attached to it—too proprietary, to the exclusion of the writer and his ideal purpose in sharing it. The first attempt to get rid of Juliana can be seen as an effort to transcend the text by degrading it—selling the girl like a mere thing. This is a failure because for Eduardo, the reader, it is already something more; it is what the writer gave, and the reader wants the text because through it he hopes for communion with the writer. The one who finally murders the text is the writer, who has done it in the very manner of his narration. The reader is grateful in the end, meeting the writer in a supra-textual aesthetic embrace—the kind which the Gutre girl did not give Espinosa. The last line of "La intrusa" tells us that what finally links the brothers is their obligation to forget Juliana. In the English version made by Borges and Norman Thomas di Giovanni (*The Aleph and Other Stories* [New York, 1970]) "obligación" is rendered as "common need."

137

It has often been noted that Borges writes a story and then a counter-story. If we indulge the idea that in some he is writing about readers who murder the literal value of a text in order to reach higher ones, we can look for another in which the idea is somehow reversed. I suggest "El indigno" (*Brodie*), whose title is almost a giveaway; I take it as a story about unworthy literature that has no aesthetic possibilities. To save time I will interpret the details as I tell them. A young Jew named Fischbein is a self-confessed coward who admires a criminal, Ferrari, because he seems brave. Fischbein follows Ferrari for a time, somewhat as the Gutres followed Espinosa; he hopes, I infer, that he will be able to reach, through Ferrari, the transcendent courage he longs for, just as a reader hopes to find aesthetic fulfillment through literature. At one point Fischbein tries to negate his text; he denies that he knows Ferrari, just as the big fisherman Peter denied knowing Christ although he believed in his transcendent, divine identity. (The allusion to Peter is not explicit; there is only the Jew, the name Fischbein, and the denial itself.) Fischbein is finally disappointed in his idol when he realizes that Ferrari is not really brave; his bravado is cowardice. Knowing of a robbery Ferrari is about to commit, Fischbein betrays him to the police and he is killed. The metallic solidity of this unworthy text is implied in its name, Ferrari.

The *Brodie* stories appeared after a lapse of a dozen years in Borges' fictional production that was caused by his going blind around 1955. Their style differs from that of his older, more complex fiction and his plots are more related to real life, but his inner metaphors and allusions are still literary, perhaps even more so than before. Noteworthy in the four stories discussed above—a factor perhaps distinguishing them from others in *Brodie*—is the repeated insinuation of the relationship between God and man through Christ as the parallel of that between writer and reader through the text. Allusions to Christ represent him as the cause of both unity and division, like Juliana of "La intrusa." I have already spoke of Juliana and Espinosa as Christ figures. In "El otro duelo" one of the rival gauchos owns a sheepdog—an *ovejero* or shepherd—named Thirty-three. When the other gaucho kills the dog, the hatred that unites the two is intensified. Also in that story we see an inversion of the triangular relationship of "La intrusa," with the Christ figure again central. There is a woman named Serviliana (apparently a combination of "servile" and "Juliana") who gives her sexual favors to both men and is later rejected by both; unlike Juliana, who was a love-link, Serviliana is a hate-link and the two men refuse to share her—an expression of the hatred they find meaningful.

The use of the analogy between Christ and the literary text as a background metaphor makes it a shadowy criterion of logic which, as Borges has shown in his essay "El arte narrativo y la magia," substitutes for objective reality as it is laboriously simulated in realism. The same kind of "magical causality" is visible in Borges' older fiction where instead of using Christ to signify literature he seems to insinuate, for example, Plato and Aristotle—or their ideas—to suggest art or thought. "Emma Zunz" (*El Aleph* [1949]) will illustrate the point. Emma's father has been wrongly dishonored by Loewenthal and has killed himself. Emma wants to kill Loewenthal in the name of justice, and the details of the story force the reader to search for a secret definition of that word—a background logic that will explain why Emma, in order to achieve her goal, must first have sexual intercourse with a stranger, to her profound disgust. The story never tells us that she wanted clinical evidence of the sexual abuse she would later allege against the murdered Loewenthal, and no detail suggests it, nor is there any hint that she needed to feel outraged in order to pull the trigger. Borges' usual allusive details, too numerous to summarize here, lead the reader to interpret "justice" as the logical consistency of conceptual forms. Emma's father is a dishonored person, and to kill in his name is to kill while standing in his Platonic category; Emma must also be a dishonored person. Once she enters her father's archetypal class, Emma *is* her father in the eyes of Plato. John Sturrock (*Paper Tigers* [Oxford, 1977]) offers the same interpretation, saying that Emma is avenging "not this or that dishonour . . . but dishonour itself, the word rather than the thing." It is well worth noting that Borges' allusions often extend to the smallest particulars, including typography. To symbolize the symmetry required for the evocation of a transcending form he often uses the alphabet. James Ashton, in "The Esthetics of Uncertainty in the Fictions of Borges" (Diss. Univ. of Texas 1980, p. 169), comments that Emma's father Emmanuel Zunz (MM, ZZ) changes his name to Manuel Maier (MM) after being ruined by Aaron (AA) Loewenthal. Emma's MM puts her in the middle between A and Z, where her father was when he killed himself. However these letters may be fitted in, they at least point to the ideality of the whole scheme of background logic.

There are other stories in the *Brodie* collection which, although they do not metaphorize the ideal reader and writer as murderers of the text, exemplify the necessity of abandoning the pretense of realism in favor of "magical causality," which in itself is a "murder" of reality for the sake of literature's magic, centrally present in metaphor. Take, for example, the metonymical metaphor. "Juan Muraña" (*Brodie*) is about a woman who is confident that her husband, a dead knife-fighter, will deliver her from a heartless landlord. It turns out that her "husband" is Juan Muraña's famous knife, with which the landlord is killed. By whom? We know it was the woman herself; but the story seems to say: Why yield to prosaic realism? Why not believe, with Shakespeare, that the evil men do lives after them—still resident in their tools? It is much more interesting than a poor woman's psychosis. Psychosis is not magic, but an animated knife performs magical feats; it reminds us of the nature of thought and language, of the intrinsic beauty of symbolism. Language reduces a farm worker to a *hand*, and an Indian soldier to one of the Bengal *Rifles*, telling us their functional significance. This is metaphor; this is literature.

"El encuentro" (*Brodie*) is a more imaginative example of the magic of metonym. Two friends get drunk at a gentleman's party and pick a fight. In their drunken state they do the unthinkable; seizing a couple of knives that once belonged to a pair of notorious duelists, they begin to spar with each other, not meaning any real harm. But the enmity inherent in the weapons takes control, they fight with inexplicable skill, and one is killed. It makes a kind of crazy logic to say that the two drunks were only the tools of the blood-thirsting steel. Literary magic, of course, is only a matter of applying in the objective order principles which are purely mental, and to transcend or "murder" the text is only to realize that however much it simulates outer reality, it is really pointing to the mind. These stories from the *Brodie* collection, as well as "Emma Zunz" and many others from Borges, are stories about imagination, the way we think—stories about the art of fiction.

Borges' view that aesthesia is without cerebral content has been made clear in his essays, conversations, and the prologues to his works.[1] This translates into the view that the only real meaning of a work is that art has occurred. In philosophical writing, or in "committed" literature (which Borges has refused to write, with minor exceptions), meaning is synonymous with practical consequences—with the text's implications for human behavior or belief. But in Borges' kind, meaning excludes all "therefores." For him art is its own purpose, its own result, its own cause and effect, and ultimately its own subject. To "murder" the text is to strip away all pretense of anything more than this—to admit that the text does not finally say anything. If it could, without ceasing to be art, it could only say "I am art and not reality."

There is a parable in the story "Guayaquil" (*Brodie*) about a pair of competing minstrels. One sings a lengthy song and hands the harp to the second. When the second merely lays it aside, the first admits defeat. Borges wants his reader to have what lies beyond the words and music, beyond the last idea. He has often said that he cannot identify a generic distinction between the Muse and the Holy Spirit.[2]

Notes

1. See the Prólogo in *Obra poética, 1923–1967* (Buenos Aires, 1964): "El sabor de la manzana (declara Berkeley) está en el contacto de la fruta con el paladar, no en la fruta misma; analógicamente (diría yo) la poesía está en el comercio del poema con el lector, no en la serie de símbolos. . . . La literatura impone su magia por artificios; el lector acaba por reconocerlos y desdeñarlos" (p. 10). Also the untitled prologue to the 3rd edition of *Elogio de la sombra* (Buenos Aires, 1969): "El hecho estético sólo puede ocurrir cuando lo escriben o lo leen" (p. 10). Borges adds that the mere use of a certain verse form tells the reader that "la emoción poética, no la información o el razonamiento, es lo que está esperándolo" (p. 10).

2. See the Prólogo (*Obra poética*): "Los griegos invocaban la musa, los hebreos el Espíritu Santo; el sentido es el mismo" (p. 12). Also the Foreword to Ronald Christ's *The Narrow Act* ([New York, 1969], p. ix), where Borges speaks of "variations on the old concept of the Holy Ghost or the Muse."

David William Foster

I

The quantity of criticism that has appeared in recent years on Borges' writings is overwhelming, and the critic who opts to add one more paper to the long list must necessarily experience a certain futility. This is especially true in the case of papers on Borges' fiction. Whereas there has been no detailed study of his essays and whereas his poetry has only recently attracted monographic attention, the stories—to a great extent the cornerstone of his international fame—have understandably merited the closest study.[1] Indeed, the number of papers on the essential aspects of the stories is great enough to warrant a bibliographic study that would attempt to abstract from them some general lines of critical reaction.

This paper would justify itself on the basis of an orientation which is somewhat removed from the thematic preoccupations which have characterized the bulk of Borgian criticism. Although Borges may have declared himself "tired of labyrinths," a reference to one of the most discussed aspects of his two major collections of stories, *Ficciones* [1944] and *El Aleph* [1949],[2] the fact remains that the audacity and the originality of his contributions to the short story have been such that criticism has, not surprisingly, focused on certain quintessential aspects of the works in an attempt to define them. In this case, the definitions proposed have centered on the figure of the labyrinth, the implications of the rejection of time, the cyclical nature of human experience, the solipsistic fallacy of both fiction and philosophy as practiced in the West, the futility but at the same time the inevitability of man's "culturism"—his creation of cultures and cultural institutions both to define and to justify himself—and the oppressive sense of "existential" terror which befalls ego-centered man as he awakens to the preceding.[3] All of these aspects constitute at least an intellectual fascination for

Modern Fiction Studies 19, No. 3 (1973): 341–51. ©1973 by Purdue Research Foundation, West Lafayette, Indiana. Reprinted by permission.

the reader of Borges' stories, and certainly the success of the latter among an international reading audience attests to the writer's artistic ability to make literature out of them. The thematic, but only occasionally rhetorical, analyses of Borges' works have been necessitated, one understands, by both their artistic complexity and their revolutionary, critical attitude toward rigidified, fossilized patterns of Western thought in both philosophy and art.

Nevertheless, it is time for a critical approach to Borges' fictions which would stress their implied poetics, the underlying, and, of course, vis-à-vis the author, probably unconscious, esthetic and rhetorical principles.[4] My interest in this paper is in seeing the Borgian poetics—and let me stress that I will assume throughout that it is indeed implied and/or unconscious—as the realization of principles that are directly related to (European) structuralism. I see two fundamental problems for the critic and his audience here. In the first place, a high percentage of literary scholars continues to subscribe to what was at an early critical moment defined as the "genetic" and the "intentional" fallacies, a fact attested to by the considerable weight attached to interviewing Borges concerning his work (the fact that Borges rarely if ever will discuss his work directly and has been known to mock gently overly-direct questions has deterred the interviewers not at all). There is little that I can say to these critics concerning my initial assumption of poetics by unconscious implication. Structuralism has only recently arrived, whereas Borges has been writing fiction since the thirties. Although one could easily trace the ancestry of current structuralist principles back to De Saussure, the Russian Formalists, and the Prague School of the first third of this century, the fact remains that, as far as literature is concerned, Latin American literature in particular, any coincidence of interest between the poets and the spokesmen of structuralism has been of only the most recent vintage. Yet the fact remains that intellectual movements are a conscious concretization of on-going trends, and any recognition of a coherent pattern at a particular moment presupposes a movement toward that pattern over a certain period of immediately previous time. That Borges' fiction had for so long before the critically conscious moment of the sixties attracted such interest for its apparently total rupture with established literary values and principles explains to a great degree how we can see him as having sensed, *avant la lettre*, the esthetic potential of structuralist principles. That Borges is grudgingly admired by the major figures of the current

Latin American literary scene, the dominant Spanish voices of the Third World, despite his political conservatism and his persistent refusal even to recognize a literature of commitment, attests to his acceptance as a bellwether of current literary esthetics.[5] Moreover, his enthusiastic reception in France (one will recall that he was "discovered" by Roger Caillois when the latter resided in Buenos Aires during the war) can hardly be the result of any essential divergence between the principles of his art and the intellectual attitudes currently in vogue.

The second problem concerns the relationship between a conscious, well-articulated (albeit confusingly multi-faceted) intellectual position and the potentially unconscious, possibly anti-intellectual principles of a writer's poetics. It goes without saying that intellectual principles, when they make the transition from "philosophy" to art, rarely survive intact. Witness the relationship between the philosopher's concept of Renaissance neoplatonism and the widely distorted ways in which it is realized in works of a primarily artistic nature. It would, of course, be naive to fault an artist for his misconceptions of intellectual or philosophical principles, but these principles are necessarily subjugated to artistic necessities, which explains why it is difficult to use, say Spanish Baroque literature, to construct an intellectual model of the Spanish Counter-Reformation. By the same token, if any concepts of structuralism in the sixties became incorporated in literary esthetics (and we have the fiction, to name a few, of Cortázar, García Márquez, Vargas Llosa, Carlos Fuentes, Cabrera Infante to serve as points of departure), we cannot expect it to be structuralism in any dogmatic or canonical sense.[6] In the case of Borges, to the extent that the implied poetics of his fiction, beginning with his first significant stories in the late thirties, may reflect at least some of the same concerns as those of the structuralists and of younger writers more directly conscious of current intellectual movements, we can only say that we have that much more the case of a writer who has been working along the same lines as the philosophers, without the concrete example of cause-and-effect that would be more essential to *la littérature comparée*. Borges and structuralism have "arrived," and any coincidence between them bespeaks the broadly-based validity of recognizing the latter as a distinct intellectual and cultural attitude and the justification of seeing the former as a central spokesman of some very contemporary problems, problems which he recognized and fictionalized well before the mainstream of our culture was able to recognize them.

II

The foregoing comments have been assuming a necessary prior knowledge on the part of the reader of the basic concerns of structuralism. We cannot review those concerns here, although specific issues will be raised as appropriate in the following discussion of Borges' implied poetics as it emerges from his fictional works. Suffice it here to refer to two major concerns which I consider primordial, at least as far as Borges' works and fiction in Latin America in the sixties have been concerned.[7] The first major concern, which underlies the so-called neoformalism of contemporary Latin American writing, is precisely the principle of structure, be it an unknown or barely sensed structure of the universe/society/human experience which the artist as man must discover and portray adequately, or be it a structure which man out of despair and solipsism creates, an act of will which imposes cosmos on chaos. An intermediate circumstance, one which is paradigmatic of the relationship between the work of art and "reality," is the creation of a structure (i.e., the work of art) which is not a documentary, naturalistic reflection of the structure of the universe, but which is a symbolic— mythic—version of it, at least as the artist, again as man, senses and interprets it (however erroneously) at that moment. The result of this attitude is an agreement that there may be divine or cosmic structures beyond human comprehension, or ones which are barely perceptible to man; that there may be structures to human society and experience which are also beyond definitive comprehension but which are barely perceptible to it; and, finally, that man may engage in the conscious and unconscious creation of structures as part of an attempt both to explain the former structures and to overcome them. As unconscious structures, we might cite our socio-cultural institutions; as conscious structures we might cite our autonomously and deliberately patterned works of art.

The second major concern, which derives immediately from the first, involves a recognition of the tentative, incomplete, arbitrary, and, ultimately, invalid nature of the structures created by man. A persistent preoccupation of modern literature, one which I can trace back to the turn of the century in Latin American poetry at least, involves the artist's realization of his inevitable failure as a vatic seer. The metaliterary concern of Borges' poetry with the inability to write the "ultimate" poem has been studied, and Borges has repeatedly spoken of the multiple products of an artist as his failures to produce the one work which will express what must be expressed. Each work is an attempt to produce the one work, the artistic Aleph, that will contain the final vision of mankind; but each attempt is the failure to achieve that ideal, and the artist abandons the previous work and undertakes the next one, always with the illusory hope of success and yet with the full knowledge that it cannot be done. There are no absolute structures, or, if there are, man is incapable of perceiving and communicating them.[8] With this, we are close to Lévi-Strauss' affirmation that the mythic patterns of a society are arbitrary and that the spiraling nature of myths represents but the vain attempt to discover the most perfect pattern of expression. For Borges, this same intuition explains the multiplicity of man's philosophical and theological systems, systems which are so wildly contradictory but which are also so enthusiastically adhered to by the true believers that he can only justify their vitality, and the vitality of the human process which continues to create new systems, in terms of the most rigorous relativism that sees all systems as ultimately vacuous and false. For Borges, from his earliest fiction, "metaphysics is a branch of fantastic literature." And as far as literature is concerned, both its multiplicity and its creative vitality bespeak, in the last analysis, its relativeness and its inadequacy ever to attain the "final" word. Although Borges continues to write, acknowledging the imperiousness of the human necessity ever to be creating new structures, his political and cultural conservatism and his early denunciation of *entre-guerre* literary vanguardism (of which he had been a leader in Argentina) are the inevitable result of his realization of the complete arbitrariness of the solutions—the structures—which man creates for his entertainment as well as for his solace.

III

Turning now to Borges' stories, we can see a definite pattern of expression of these two major concerns, as well as of the other issues which have been articulated within structuralism, in his two major collections, *Ficciones* and *El Aleph*. (Thirty-four stories are involved in these two collections; *El informe de Brodie* [1970] claims to abandon entirely the poetics of the first two collections, but whether this is the case or not must be the subject of an independent study.) My approach will be typological and in terms of a trajectory of principles which from one point of view could be called purely intellectual, but which from the point of view of the stories themselves—from the point of view of autonomously structured art—represent a coherent poetics which has served, I propose, as the very basis for the rhetorical structure of those stories. I realize that in discussing the stories in these terms, the emphasis falls more directly on a putative typology or trajectory which it is claimed that they manifest in terms of an implied esthetic. That is to say, I am forced to assume that the individual stories, as autonomous works of literary art, do not need any further elucidation, that we as readers agree basically on their "meaning," and that, as "known" elements, they can be used for the purposes of tracing certain common patterns between them.

Borges, from one of his earliest stories, established his concern for the creative process of man's mind. In "Tlön, Uqbar, Orbis Tertius," one of his most widely discussed stories, he presents the vast and troubling prospect of a series of enterprises to create fictitious realms, each vaster than the last, realms which, by virtue of the intensity of the enterprise, ultimately impose themselves materially upon the "real" world. Jaime Alazraki has recently discussed this story in terms of contemporary concepts of history and cultural institutions,[9] and it is now possible to see this early, "cardinal" story of Borges', which initially was taken as proof of his ascetic, pseudo-philosophical preoccupations, as the elaboration of an ironic vision of man's intellectual constructs—theology, philosophy, history, mathematics, and, of course, literature—as the creation of virtually empty, *ad hoc* systems which he eventually comes to take—to mistake—for reality itself. That objects from the fictitious Uqbar appear in the real world is a hyperbolic indication of how our intellectual games (the spirit in which the realm was conceived) become so real for us: man commits the solipsism of believing that his rational schemata do, in fact, correspond to those of the universe; *are*, in fact, those of the universe.[10]

Although it has not been adequately commented on, the narrative voice of the story is perhaps the most significant indication of the importance of the "revelations" which it contains. A first-person narrator, called Borges, relates in tones of amusement, then awe, and finally despair, the discovery of the projects relating to the fictitious realms. At the end of the story, convinced within himself that the tangible world which he knows (the beloved, semi-rural Argentine society of his ancestors) is to be supplanted by the unchecked fantasies of those who "game" at creating philosophies and worlds, he retires to the seclusion of a provincial hotel and minor literary pursuits. The implication is clearly a metaphysical anguish in the face of man's creative drives and the imperiousness with which his creations—new myths by which he comes to live unswervingly—become all-consuming passions. Of course, what Borges has to say about *ad hoc* philosophical systems here applies equally to art (not much before this story Borges had disassociated himself from the vanguard poetic dogma of the period, which was being espoused with truculent, quasi-religious fervor). That his first major collection, of which "Tlön" is the lead story, is called *Ficciones*—*Fictions*, which evokes in Spanish the etymologically related verb "to feign"—is not insignificant in this context.[11] Most, if not all, of the stories deal with fictional constructs—philosophies, books, labyrinths, lotteries, detective solutions—and the stories are themselves, in turn, fictional constructs, stories which, as Borges has said repeatedly, reveal the monotony and the simple-mindedness of their author as a man and as an artist. That monotony is, precisely, the fascination with man's need to create fictions—myths—and the attempt of the artist, by the same token, to create a correspondingly symbolic or metaphoric fiction to describe and to interpret this need.

The idea of a *one*, of a universal symbol, a perfect philosophy or myth, of an Ultimate Book that will contain all the others and be the final key to the universe—of a Bible, in short—is manifest in several works. In the title story of *El Aleph*, we have an ironic vision of that search. That it is a quest for the truth concerning an amorous relationship only increases the irony. The narrator's final comprehension comes via a hoax over an *aleph*, a point in the universe that contains all other points, a symbol of ultimate mystical vision or knowledge. The hoax, of course, bespeaks the illusory nature of the quest, whereas the possibility of the perpetration of the hoax (which becomes multifaceted in Borges' typically complicated fictional elaboration) underlines man's innate drive to discover the *alephs* that will justify and explain him.[12] In the early story "La biblioteca de Babel," another first-person narrator describes the universe in terms of a vast library— a literal Tower of Babel—in which the inhabitants, the librarians, search frantically and in vain for the One Book that they are convinced must exist.[13]

On the other hand, in "La lotería en Babilonia" the first-person narrator, who is unexplainably afforded an absence from Babilonia— *i.e.*, afforded a circumstance of objectivity—describes his people's evolution of a lottery system which endows their existence with the aura of mysterious and transcendent fulfillment. The lottery, as it is described, is nothing more nor less than the perfect imitation of the arbitrary, random, existential chaos of human existence, and the lottery, in its slow evolution, has unwittingly moved from a causal, "logical," mechanism to one which has essentially merged and become confused with a stoic conception of the lot of man. Significantly, the narrator does not indicate his realization of this detail and at the end tells his unidentified interlocutor that the boat is ready to take him back to Babilonia, back to the "ordered lottery" of that microcosm. Although there is little explicit support for it, I cannot help feeling that this story is also metaphorical of the process of fiction, both on the external level of man's creation of systems as well as on the internal level of the artist's creation of literary artifices.[14] The story, like the narrator's monologue, is a momentary ordered circumstance which has been afforded him to "explain things," after which both narrator and writer must return to the random lottery of existence. The lottery, the explanation of it, and the ordered story which reports the explanation become confused, thanks in great part to the troubled urgency of the narrator's tone, as simply interlocking fictions that may have a persuasive ring of truth about them, but which are, *mutatis mutandis*, the universal feignings of fiction. In this context one might also mention the story "Los teólogos," which concerns the brutal competition between two theologians for the acceptance of the commentaries of one and the discreditation of those of the other. The battle is waged with all the violent skills of academic feuding, and one of the theologians is condemned to the stake. But the triumphant theologian, the narrator (who in the story is the omniscient reporter) gives us to understand, must discover in death that, not only are the discrepancies between the commentaries of the two meaningless, but that in all probability God is not even aware of the bitter and brutal struggle for "truth" which has been waged in His name. Clearly, the implication is that man's blind adherence to his systems, an adherence which would deliver up to the flames those who do not agree with those systems, is based on the false but tenacious assumption that those systems do, in fact, possess divine meaning. Unfortunately, as the cynical and ironic stance of Borges' narrators—both first- and third-person—so vividly demonstrates, man will continue to create his systems, will continue to adhere to them blindly, in his mysterious and urgent quest for divine justification and comprehension. The vacuousness of his symbols, of his systems, even when he is vaguely aware of this fact, does not deter him from his quest. The artist, Borges, whose stories enunciate this vision of man's quest and the symbols of that quest, is correspondingly undeterred from his urgent compounding of fictions that are, in the last analysis, only fictional metaphors of the same quest and its validity, or lack of it. The stories are no more nor less true than any of man's systems, which explains—and justifies—to a great extent the aura of irreality and divine deceit, true objective narrative correlatives, with which the storyteller invests them.

IV

One might well ask at this point how what I have said up until now differs from the numerous—the almost innumerable—discussions of Borges, his stories, and their meaning. How, in other words, does the preceding have to do with a structuralist poetics and not simply with a thematics, the latter understandably the most overworked critical focus on the Argentine's fiction. Aside from the facile observation that there is no critically or theoretically justifiable distinction between poetics and thematics, any adequate answer to this supposed demand must be based on an understanding of the peculiar relationship between the vision of the stories and their status as autonomous literary structures. I have mentioned repeatedly and insistently how many of the stories establish a tone of urgency and awe or despair vis-à-vis their own revelations. This is accomplished frequently by means of a first-person narrator who is essentially reporting his own personal experience, although on occasion a third-person, an omniscient reporter or a by-stander (often in the form of a curious bibliophile) may report the experience of others. Obsessively, therefore, the stories of *Ficciones* and *El Aleph* give rhetorical shape or structure to, precisely, individuals' or peoples' quest to give shape or structure to their intuitions, false or divine, concerning human experience. Borges has been repeatedly attacked for seeing man in terms of his cultural constructs—his "philosophies" and his institutions—rather than in perhaps the more voguish terms of his inner existential or outer sociological circumstances. But obviously for Borges, the latter are also constructs, cultural ones in the broadest sense, and he sees man as obsessed by these constructs, be they either his own immediate fabrication or the fabrication of "divinities"—social, political, cultural forces—beyond his immediate grasp. But the stories too are necessarily constucts; literary art is, by definition, an *ad hoc* structure, an immediate and conscious giving shape to the word (hence, Borges' title, *El hacedor—The Maker*—for his 1960

151

collection of prose and poetry, many of which pieces deal explicitly with the ontology of literature).

In his story, "La busca de Averroes," Borges is concerned directly with the relationship between the immediate structure of his fictional artifice and the structure of the quest of the protagonist. The title of the story is significantly ambiguous and can mean either "The Search by Averroes/Averroes' Search" or "The Search for Averroes/In Search of Averroes." The main body of the story deals ironically, almost comically, with the philosopher's search for the definition of "tragedy" and "comedy" as used by Aristotle, the famous commentary on whose works Averroes is seen engaged in writing. Averroes, we know from our western point of view in the twentieth century, fails in his search, even though we see his pleasure at having discovered, so he thinks, the meaning of the two mysterious words in the Greek text. Abruptly, the narrator shifts to a discussion of himself and of the curious inappropriateness of the ironical tone of his description of Averroes' erroneous conclusions. For, he asks, is not his own search for a definition of Averroes and his search just as illusory, just as ironically erroneous as Averroes' search for the meaning of Aristotle's terminology? Via his metacommentary,[15] Borges has both defined the precarious nature of his personal literary structure, as well as demonstrated the direct relationship which it has with the nature of the structures—the myths, if one will—by which mankind satisfies itself. It is in this sense that we are speaking of what may be called a thematics, but what is, by virtue of its metacommentary nature and its correspondence to the questions of fictional rhetoric, also most assuredly a poetics as well.

Notes

1. The best single monographic study which I can recommend on Borges' fiction is Carter Wheelock, *The Mythmaker, a Study of Motif and Symbol in the Short Stories of Jorge Luis Borges* (Austin: University of Texas Press, 1969). Wheelock sees Borges' stories as multiple examples of the attempt to create stories of mythic proportions while at the same time questioning that very attempt. They are, in short, metaliterary exercises. To the extent that Wheelock sees the stories dealing with the nature of art, his frame of reference is close to my own although he is more interested in straight thematics than in issues of structure.

2. See the interview with César Fernández Moreno, originally published in Spanish but available in English as "Weary of Labyrinths: An Interview with Jorge Luis Borges," *Encounter*, 32, 4 (1969), 3–14. The figure of the labyrinth attains its most perfect form in *El Aleph*. See the article by L. A. Murillo, "The Labyrinths of Jorge Luis Borges, an Introductory [sic] to the Stories of *The Aleph*," *Modern Language Quarterly*, 20 (1959), 259–266, and the follow-up by Frank Dauster, "Notes on Borges' Labyrinths," *Hispanic Review*, 30 (1962), 142–148.

3. The best survey of Borges' themes is Jaime Alazraki, *La prosa narrativa de Jorge Luis Borges* (Madrid: Gredos, 1968).

4. Some suggestions have been made concerning Borges' esthetics as revealed in his essays on other works of literature. See Thomas A. Hart, Jr., "The Literary Criticism of Jorge Luis Borges," *MLN*, 78 (1963), 489–503, and Emir Rodríguez-Monegal, "Borges como crítico literario," *La palabra y el hombre*, No. 31 (1964), 411–416. Both focus on the question of Crocean influence (pro and con, respectively).

5. From the outset of his career in fiction, Borges has been attacked vehemently for his "sins." The attacks crystallized in the fifties at the time of the emergence of an existentially committed criticism, which took on, so to speak, Borges' solid reputation. See Adolfo Prieto, *Borges y la nueva generación* (Buenos Aires: Letras Universitarias, 1954). Other major figures of the moment grudgingly admit his brilliance and perhaps even his revolutionary achievements in literature, if not in his social deportment. Nevertheless and although he is able to refrain from denouncing his politics, Fernando Alegría, in his recent collection of essays on the Latin American writer and his commitment to his society and its problems, can only barely bring himself to mention Borges: *Literatura y revolución* (México: Fondo de Cultura Económica, 1971). On the other hand, concerning the enthusiastic reception of the French, see the large volume of homage studies published by *Cahiers de L'Herne*, No. 4 (1964). Ariel Dorfman is especially just in recognizing Borges' interest in violence, one of the major concerns of Latin American cultural revolutionaries: "Borges y la

violencia americana," in his *Imaginación y violencia en América* (Santiago de Chile: Editorial Universitaria, 1970), pp. 38–64.

6. This point is emphasized in my paper on structuralism and the Peruvian novelist Mario Vargas Llosa: "Consideraciones estructurales sobre 'La Casa Verde,' " *Norte*, 12 (1971), 128–136.

7. Many major texts of European structuralism have become available in English and Spanish, and in their latter version they have had an enthusiastic reception in the major intellectual centers of Latin America, Buenos Aires in particular. I would recommed the following in particular: Octavio Paz, *Claude Lévi-Strauss o el nuevo festín de Esopo* (México: Joaquín Mortiz, 1967, recently made available in English by Cornell University Press); José Sazbón, *Estructuralismo y literatura* (Buenos Aires: Nueva Visión, 1970); Jean Piaget, *Structuralism* (New York: Basic Books, 1970); Michael Lane, *Introduction to Structuralism* (New York: Basic Books, 1970); Jacques Ehrmann, *Structuralism* (Garden City, N.Y.: Doubleday, 1970); Eugenio Donato, "Of Structuralism and Literature," *MLN*, 82 (1967), 549–574. Carlos Fuentes has brought concepts of structuralism to his study of contemporary Latin American novelists: *La nueva novela hispanoamericana* (México: Joaquín Mortiz, 1969).

8. Cf. Borges' famous assertion in the epilogue to *El hacedor* (1960; *Dreamtigers* in English): "Un hombre se propone la tarea de dibujar el mundo. A lo largo de los años puebla un espacio con imágenes de provincias, de reinos, de montañas, de bahías, de naves, de islas, de peces, de habitaciones, de instrumentos, de astros, de caballos, y de personas. Poco antes de morir, descubre que ese paciente laberinto de líneas traza la imagen de su cara." It is not even necessary for these lines to be placed as an epilogue to a collection of prose and poetry for them to be taken as tantamount to a refutation of any objective accomplishments for the writer's art. Lewis H. Rubman has discussed in a fine article the question of "artistic doubt" in poetry: "Los límites del arte en algunos poemas de Borges," *Mundo nuevo*, No. 32 (1969), 55–65.

9. Jaime Alazraki, "Tlön y Asterión: anverso y reverso de una epistemología," *Nueva narrativa hispanoamericana*, 1, 2, (1971), 21–33.

10. Concerning Borges' skepticism vis-à-vis man's intellectual games, a skepticism which resolves itself in terms of fiction being the only valid exercise of man's intelligence, see Frances Weyers Weber, "Borges's Stories: Fiction and Philosophy," *Hispanic Review*, 36 (1968), 124–141.

11. Concerning the unity of this collection and what I would call its metaliterary features, see Noé Jitrik, "Estructura y significado en *Ficciones* de Jorge Luis Borges," *Casa de las Américas*, No. 53 (1969), 50–62. In terms of the attitudes mentioned in note 5, that this enthusiastic and profound article was published in the organ of the official cultural agency, the Casa de las Américas, of the Castro government stands witness to the increased sophistication and objectivity of Latin American leftist criticism.

12. See the discussions of the story by Alberto J. Carlos, "Dante y 'El

Aleph' de Borges" *Duquesne Hispanic Review*, 5 (1966), 35–50; and Cándido Pérez Gallego, "El descubrimiento de la realidad en 'El Aleph' de Jorge Luis Borges," *Cuadernos hispanoamericanos*, No. 214 (1967), 186–193.

13. Borges has written elsewhere in his essays on the cultural and "mythical" significance of books in libraries, particularly in the collection *Otras inquisiciones* (1952; *Other Inquisitions* in English). See in particular the essay "El culto de los libros."

14. Although he does not come to quite as strong a conclusion, Neil D. Isaacs perceives the relationship between Borges' "intellectual figures" such as the labyrinth and art: "The Labyrinth of Art in Four *Ficciones* of Jorge Luis Borges," *Studies in Short Fiction*, 6 (1969), 383–394. Concerning the self-conscious artifice of Borges' art, see Patricia Merivale, "The Flaunting of Artifice in Vladimir Nabokov and Jorge Luis Borges," *Wisconsin Studies in Contemporary Literature*, 8 (1967); 294–309.

15. I am using "metacommentary" here with reference to literature as Fredric Jameson uses it in reference to criticism in "Metacommentary," *PMLA*, 86 (1971), 9–18.

Chronology

1899   Jorges Luis Borges born in Buenos Aires to Jorge Borges and Leonor Acevedo de Borges; his father's English mother, as well as a library in English, provides a bilingual environment.

1914–1919   Family resides in Switzerland; Borges cultivates lifelong interest in Germanic-language literatures.

1919   Family leaves Switzerland for Spain, where Borges becomes involved with avant-garde Ultraísta movement.

1921   Returns to Buenos Aires; influenced by Macedonio Fernández and this thinker's radically innovative literary concepts. Becomes a leader of Buenos Aires avant-garde.

1923–1929   Establishes a reputation as an experimental poet with three collections of avant-garde verse; as a controversial critic, broadens the Argentine public's literary tastes.

1930   Now a detractor of avant-gardism, cultivates a distanced, ironic expression. Moves away from poetry; experiments with giving his essays elements of imaginative writing; as critic, urges appreciation of nonrealistic narratives and parables.

1933   Magazine *Megáfono* runs a lengthy feature in which major Argentine writers and critics join in controversy over Borges.

1935   Publishes *A Universal History of Infamy*, brief biographical essays that incorporate features of short fiction; includes "Streetcorner Man," a fairly conventional short story.

1936   *History of Eternity*, otherwise a collection of essays, contains the now-famous "The Approach to al-Mu'tasim," the first fully realized example of Borges's baroque, ambiguously symbolic short fiction, with many features of the essay; this story is later incorporated into *Ficciones*.

157

1938   Father dies; under financial exigency, assumes librarian post; suffers near-fatal aftereffects from accident on 24 December.

1939   Convalescent, makes what he later recalls as a momentous shift toward being a writer of short stories; after this decision, writes "Pierre Menard, Author of *Don Quixote*."

1940   With Bioy Casares and Silvina Ocampo publishes the famous anthology of fantastic literature *The Book of Fantasy*, promoting the three friends' ideal of imaginative, nonmimetic short fiction.

1941   *The Garden of Forking Paths* is the first collection of short stories in Borges' oblique, intricately symbolic mode.

1942   With Adolfo Bioy Casares, publishes *Six Problems for Don Isidro Parodi*, detective stories barbed with mockery; the authors share the pseudonym H. Bustos Domecq and a joint approach to short fiction unlike their individual literary modes. The magazine *Sur* dedicates a special issue to Borges.

1943   With Bioy Casares, publishes *The Best Detective Stories*, setting taste for precisely constructed, stylized tales of detection.

1944   *Ficciones (1935–1944)*, adding six new stories to the 1941 collection, becomes the author's most important book. Wins Prize of Honor from Argentine Society of Writers.

1946–1955   General Juan Domingo Perón becomes Argentina's president; Borges runs afoul of Perón and his career suffers as a result.

1949   *The Aleph* contains more convoluted, symbolically encoded short fiction; it forms a pair with *Ficciones*.

1951   Gallimard publishes a French translation of *Ficciones* by P. Verdevoye and Nestor Ibarra; a Borges cult begins to grow in France.

1952   *The Aleph* reissued with five additional stories.

1953   Roger Caillois publishes *Labyrinthes* (Gallimard), stories by Borges, who is now "discovered" in Europe.

1955   Resumes a prominent place in national intellectual life following the fall of Perón. Named director of the National

Library and member of the Argentine Academy of Letters. Loss of sight becomes nearly total.

1956 Becomes Professor of English Literature at the University of Buenos Aires; wins National Prize for Literature. *Ficciones* reissued with three stories from up to 1953.

1957 *Manual of Fantastic Zoology* (with Margarita Guerrero; in later versions, *The Book of Imaginary Beings*) fully displays the author's practice of creating works in reference format with largely spurious content.

1960 Publishes *Dreamtigers*, a mix of poetry and brief prose pieces, only some of which are narrative.

1961 Wins the International Publishers' (Formentor) Prize, along with Samuel Beckett; translations of *Ficciones* are slated to appear in six literary capitals. Named Edward Laroque Tinker Visiting Professor at University of Texas at Austin. Undertakes first of many U.S. lecture tours.

1962 *Labyrinths*, a Borges miscellany (New Directions) is a surprise best-seller. Grove Press publishes *Ficciones*.

1964 Voluminous issue of *Cahiers de L'Herne* (Paris) on Borges's fiction.

1966–1970 Writes and begins to publish new short stories, his first since 1954; declares himself "weary of labyrinths"; new work is less baroque and centers on memorable plots.

1967 Named Charles Eliot Norton Lecturer at Harvard. With Bioy Casares, under joint pseudonym Bustos Domecq, publishes *Crónicas de Bustos Domecq*, satirical short fiction under the guise of book reviews by a vacuously modish art critic.

1969 *In Praise of Darkness*, otherwise verse, contains two new Borges stories, "Pedro Salvadores" and "The Anthropologist."

1970 Publishes *Doctor Brodie's Report*, whose stories mark his return to the genre and his concern with the tale-teller's art.

1971 Publishes *El congreso*, a long short story; *El Aleph* reissued with one additional story.

1975   Publishes *The Book of Sand*, more vividly plotted stories; favors ancient Nordic settings and supernatural events.

1977   Publishes last stories, with Bioy Casares: *New Stories by Bustos Domecq*, full of benevolent humor and local color.

1977–1986   Although publishing little new, maintains a role in literary life through public statements and interviews.

1986   Dies in Geneva, Switzerland.

Selected Bibliography

Primary Works

Short Fiction Collections

El Aleph. Buenos Aires: Losada, 1949 (contains "El inmortal," "El muerto," "Historia del guerrero y de la cautiva," "Biografía de Isidoro Tadeo Cruz [1829–1874]," "Emma Zunz," "La casa de Asterión," "La otra muerte," "Deutsches Requiem," "La busca de Averroes," "El Zahir," "La escritura del Dios," "El Aleph," and "Epílogo"). Buenos Aires: Losada, 1952 (also contains "Los teólogos," "Abencaján el Bojarí, muerto en su laberinto," "Los dos reyes y los dos laberintos," "La espera," and "El hombre en el umbral"). Buenos Aires: Emecé, 1957. Barcelona: Planeta, 1969. Madrid: Alianza, 1971 (also contains "La intrusa"). *The Aleph and Other Stories, 1933–1969, Together with Commentaries and an Autobiographical Essay.* Edited and translated by Norman Thomas di Giovanni. New York: E. P. Dutton, 1970 (contains "The Aleph," "Streetcorner Man," "The Approach to al-Mu'tasim," "The Circular Ruins," "Death and the Compass," "The Life of Tadeo Isidoro Cruz [1829–1874]," "The Two Kings and Their Two Labyrinths," "The Dead Man," "The Other Death," "Ibn Hakkan al-Bokari Dead in His Labyrinth," "The Man on the Threshold," "The Challenge," "The Captive," "Borges and Myself," "The Intruder," "The Immortals," "The Meeting," "Pedro Salvadores," "Rosendo's Tale," and selected nonfiction).
El congreso. Buenos Aires: Archibrazo Editor, 1971 (contains "El congreso"). *The Congress.* Translated by Norman Thomas di Giovanni. London: Enitharmon Press, 1974 (contains "The Congress").
Ficciones (1935–1944). Buenos Aires: Sur, 1944 (contains all the stories of *El jardín de senderos que se bifurcan*, which forms one of two subsections of *Ficciones*, plus, in the subsection designated "Artificios," "Funes el memorioso," "La forma de la espada," "Tema del traidor y del héroe," "La muerte y la brújula," "El milagro secreto," and "Tres versiones de Judas"). Buenos Aires: Emecé, 1956 (also contains "El fin," "La secta del Fénix," and "El sur"). Barcelona: Editorial Planeta/Buenos Aires: Emecé, 1971 (under title *Ficciones; relatos*). Madrid: Alianza Editorial/ Buenos Aires: Emecé, 1971. London: Harrap, 1976 (edited with an introduction by Gordon Brotherston and Peter Hulme). *Ficciones.* Edited by Anthony Kerrigan; translated by Kerrigan and others. London: Wei-

denfeld/New York: Grove Press, 1962 (contains "Tlön, Uqbar, Orbis Tertius," "The Approach to Al-Mu'tasim," "Pierre Menard, Author of *Don Quixote*," "The Circular Ruins," "The Babylon Lottery," "An Examination of the Work of Herbert Quain," "The Library of Babel," "The Garden of Forking Paths," "Funes the Memorious," "The Shape of the Sword," "The Theme of the Traitor and the Hero," "Death and the Compass," "The Secret Miracle," "Three Versions of Judas," "The End," "The Sect of the Phoenix," and "The South").

Historia universal de la infamia. Buenos Aires: Editorial Tor, 1935 (contains "El espantoso redentor Lazarus Morell," "El impostor inverosímil Tom Castro," "La viuda Ching, pirata puntual," "El proveedor de iniquidades Monk Eastman," "El asesino desinteresado Bill Harrigan," "El incivil maestro de ceremonias Kotsuké no Suké," "El tintorero enmascarado Hákim de Merv," "Hombre de la esquina rosada," and miscellaneous short prose pieces). Buenos Aires: Emecé, 1954, 1958, 1962, 1964, 1965, 1967, 1969, 1972. Madrid: Alianza, 1971, 1978. *A Universal History of Infamy.* Translated by Norman Thomas di Giovanni. New York: E. P. Dutton, 1970 (contains "The Dread Redeemer Lazarus Morell," "Tom Castro the Implausible Imposter," "The Widow Ching, Lady Pirate," "Monk Eastman, Purveyor of Iniquities," "The Disinterested Killer Bill Harrigan," "The Insulting Master of Etiquette Kotsuké no Suké," "The Masked Dyer, Hákkim of Merv," "Streetcorner Man," and miscellaneous short prose pieces).

El jardín de senderos que se bifurcan. Buenos Aires: Sur, 1941 (contains "Tlön, Uqbar, Orbis Tertius," "El acercamiento a Almotásim," "Pierre Menard, autor del Quijote," "Las ruinas circulares," "La lotería en Babilonia," "Examen de la obra de Herbert Quain," "La biblioteca de Babel," and "El jardín de senderos que se bifurcan"). *Labyrinths.* Edited by James E. Irby and Donald A. Yates; various translators. New York: New Directions, 1962 (contains "Tlön, Uqbar, Orbis Tertius," "The Lottery in Babylon," "Pierre Menard, Author of the Quixote," "The Circular Ruins," "The Library of Babel," "Funes the Memorious," "The Shape of the Sword," "Theme of the Traitor and the Hero," "Death and the Compass," "The Secret Miracle," "Three Versions of Judas," "The Sect of the Phoenix," "The Immortal," "The Theologians," "Story of the Warrior and the Captive," "Emma Zunz," "The House of Asterion," "Deutsches Requiem," "Averroes' Search," "The Zahir," "The Waiting," and selected essays and parables).

El informe de Brodie. Buenos Aires: Emecé, 1970 (contains "La intrusa," "El indigno," "Historia de Rosendo Juárez," "El encuentro," "Juan Muraña," "La señora mayor," "El duelo," "El otro duelo," "Guayaquil," "El evangelio según Marcos," and "El informe de Brodie"). Two stories from the same period of production as *El informe de Brodie*—"El etnógrafo" and "Pedro Salvadores"—were published in the otherwise verse

collection *Elogio de la sombra* ([Buenos Aires: Emecé, 1969], 59–61, 77–79). *Doctor Brodie's Report.* Translated by Norman Thomas di Giovanni. New York: E. P. Dutton, 1973 (contains "The Gospel according to Mark," "The Unworthy Friend," "The Duel," "The End of the Duel," "Rosendo's Tale," "The Intruder," "The Meeting," "Juan Muraña," "The Elder Lady," "Guayaquil," and "Doctor Brodie's Report").
El libro de arena. Buenos Aires: Emecé, 1975 (contains "El otro," "Ulrica," "El congreso," "There Are More Things," "La secta de los Treinta," "La noche de los dones," "El espejo y la máscara," "Undr," "Utopía de un hombre que está cansado," "El soborno," "Avelino Arredondo," "El disco," "El libro de arena," and "Epílogo"). *The Book of Sand.* Translated by Norman Thomas di Giovanni. New York: E. P. Dutton, 1977 (contains "The Other," "Ulrike," "The Congress," "There Are More Things," "The Sect of the Thirty," "The Night of the Gifts," "The Mirror and the Mask," "Undr," "Utopia of a Tired Man," "The Bribe," "Avelino Arredondo," "The Disk," and "The Book of Sand").

Poetry Collections
La cifra. Buenos Aires: Emecé, 1981.
Cuaderno San Martín. Buenos Aires: Editorial Proa, 1929.
Elogio de la sombra. Buenos Aires: Emecé, 1969. *In Praise of Darkness.* Translated by Norman Thomas di Giovanni. New York: E. P. Dutton, 1974.
Fervor de Buenos Aires. Buenos Aires: Private edition, 1923. Buenos Aires: Emecé, 1969.
Historia de la noche. Buenos Aires: Emecé, 1976.
Luna de enfrente. Buenos Aires: Proa, 1925.
Luna de enfrente. Cuaderno San Martín. Buenos Aires: Emecé, 1969.
La moneda de hierro. Buenos Aires: Emecé, 1976.
El oro de los tigres. Buenos Aires: Emecé, 1972. *The Gold of the Tigers, Selected Later Poems: A Bilingual Edition.* Translated by Alastair Reid. New York: E. P. Dutton, 1977. Includes selections from *La rosa profunda.*
El otro, el mismo. Buenos Aires: Emecé, 1969.
La rosa profunda. Buenos Aires: Emecé, 1975. *The Gold of the Tigers, Selected Later Poems: A Bilingual Edition.* Translated by Alastair Reid. New York: E. P. Dutton, 1977. Includes selections from *El oro de los tigres.*
Selected Poems, 1923–1967. Edited and translated with notes by Norman Thomas di Giovanni. London: A. Lane, Penguin Press, 1972. New York: Dell, 1973, 1972.

Poetry and Prose Collections
Dreamtigers. Translated by Mildred Boyer and Harold Morland. Austin: University of Texas Press, 1964. New York: E. P. Dutton, 1970.
El hacedor. Buenos Aires: Emecé, 1960.

163

Selected Bibliography

Nonfiction

Antiguas literaturas germánicas, with Delia Ingenieros. Mexico City/Buenos Aires: Fondo de Cultura Económica, 1951.

Discusión. Buenos Aires: Manuel Gleizer, 1932; rev. ed., 1957. Madrid: Alianza, 1976.

Evaristo Carriego. Buenos Aires: Manuel Gleizer, 1930. Buenos Aires: Emecé, 1955. Madrid: Alianza, 1976. *Evaristo Carriego: A Book about Old-Time Buenos Aires.* Translated with introduction and notes by Norman Thomas de Giovanni with the assistance of Susan Ashe. New York: E. P. Dutton, 1983.

Historia de la eternidad. Buenos Aires: Viau y Zona, 1936. Buenos Aires: Emecé, 1953. Madrid: Alianza/Buenos Aires: Emecé, 1971.

El idioma de los argentinos. Buenos Aires: Manuel Gleizer, 1928. Reissued in a double volume with José Edmundo Clemente, *El idioma de Buenos Aires* (Buenos Aires: Peña del Giudice, 1952).

Inquisiciones. Buenos Aires: Editorial Proa, 1925.

Leopoldo Lugones, with Betina Edelberg. Buenos Aires: Troquel, 1955. Reissued in a volume with a bibliography by Edgardo Cozarinsky (Buenos Aires: Editorial Pleamar, 1965).

El libro de los seres imaginarios, with Margarita Guerrero. Incorporates 1957 *Manual de zoología fantástica.* Buenos Aires: Kier, 1967. *The Book of Imaginary Beings.* Translated by Norman Thomas di Giovanni. New York: E. P. Dutton, 1969. Hammondsworth, England: Penguin, 1974. The Penguin version was considerably revised by Borges and di Giovanni from *El libro de los seres imaginarios.*

Literaturas germánicas medievales, with María Esther Vásquez. Incorporates 1951 *Antiguas literaturas germánicas.* Buenos Aires: Falbo Librero Editor, 1966.

Manual de zoología fantástica, with Margarita Guerrero. Mexico City/Buenos Aires: Fondo de Cultura Económica, 1957.

El "Martín Fierro," with Margarita Guerrero. Buenos Aires: Columba, 1953.

Otras inquisiciones (1937–1952). Buenos Aires: Editorial Sur, 1952. Buenos Aires: Emecé, 1960. Madrid: Alianza, 1976. *Other Inquisitions, 1937–1952.* Translated by Ruth L. C. Simms. Austin: University of Texas Press, 1964. New York: Washington Square Press, 1966. New York: Simon & Schuster, 1968. London: Souvenir Press, 1973.

El tamaño de mi esperanza. Buenos Aires: Editorial Proa, 1926.

Collaborative Fiction Collections

Crónicas de Bustos Domecq, with Adolfo Bioy Casares, under pseudonym H. Bustos Domecq. Buenos Aires: Losada, 1967. *Chronicles of Bustos Domecq.* Translated by Norman Thomas di Giovanni. New York: E. P. Dutton, 1976.

Dos fantasías memorables, with Adolfo Bioy Casares, under pseudonym H. Bustos Domecq. Buenos Aires: Oportet & Haereses, 1946.

Un modelo para la muerte, with Adolfo Bioy Casares, under pseudonym B. Suárez Lynch. Buenos Aires: Oportet & Haereses, 1946. Reissue bearing authors' real names, Buenos Aires, Edicom, 1970.

Nuevos cuentos de Bustos Domecq, with Adolfo Bioy Casares, under pseudonym H. Bustos Domecq. Buenos Aires: Ediciones Librería La Ciudad, 1977.

Seis problemas para don Isidro Parodi, with Adolfo Bioy Casares, under pseudonym H. Bustos Domecq. Buenos Aires: Ediciones Sur, 1942. *Six Problems for Don Isidro Parodi*. Translated by Norman Thomas di Giovanni. New York: E. P. Dutton, 1980.

Short Fiction Anthologies

Antología de la literatura fantástica, with Silvina Ocampo and Adolfo Bioy Casares. Buenos Aires: Sudamericana, 1940; expanded ed., 1965; reissued 1967, 1971, 1976. Barcelona: EDHASA, 1976. *The Book of Fantasy*. Introduction by Ursula K. Le Guin. New York: Penguin, 1989.

Cuentos breves y extraordinarios, antología, with Bioy Casares. Buenos Aires: Editorial Raigal, 1955. Buenos Aires: Santiago Rueda, 1967. Buenos Aires: Losada, 1973; reissued 1976. *Extraordinary Tales*. Translated by Anthony Kerrigan. New York: Herder & Herder, 1971. London: Souvenir Press, 1973.

Los mejores cuentos policiales, with Bioy Casares. Buenos Aires: Emecé, 1943; reissued 1944, 1947. Madrid: Alianza, 1972; reissued 1976, 1981.

Los mejores cuentos policiales: segunda serie, with Adolfo Bioy Casares. Buenos Aires: Emecé, 1951; reissued 1952, 1956, 1962, 1965.

Screenplay

Los orilleros. El paraíso de los creyentes, with Adolfo Bioy Casares. Buenos Aires: Emecé, 1972.

Secondary Works

Interviews

Alifano, Roberto. *Twenty-four Conversations with Borges Including a Selection of Poems: Interviews with Roberto Alifano 1981–1983*. Various translators. Housatonic, Mass.: Lascaux Publications (distributed by Grove Press), 1984.

Barnstone, Willis. *Borges at Eighty: Conversations*. Bloomington: Indiana University Press, 1982.

Burgin, Richard. *Conversations with Jorge Luis Borges*. New York: Holt, Rinehart & Winston, 1969.

Christ, Ronald. "The Art of Fiction XXXIX." *Paris Review* 10, no. 40 (Winter–Spring 1967): 116–64.

Selected Bibliography

De Milleret, Jean. *Entretiens avec Jorge Luis Borges.* Paris: Pierre Belfond, 1967.
Di Giovanni, Norman Thomas; Daniel Halpern; and Frank MacShane. *Borges on Writing.* New York: E. P. Dutton, 1973.
Fernández Moreno, César. "Harto de los laberintos." *Mundo Nuevo* [Paris], no. 18 (December 1967): 8–29. Reprinted as "Weary of Labyrinths." *Encounter* 32, no. 4 (1969): 3–14.
Guibert, Rita. "Jorge Luis Borges." In her *Seven Voices*, 75–117. New York: Knopf, 1973.
Harss, Luis. "Jorge Luis Borges o la consolación por la filosofía." In his *Los nuestros*, 128–70. Buenos Aires: Sudamericana, 1966. Translated as "Jorge Luis Borges or the Consolation by Philosophy." In *Into the Mainstream: Conversations with Latin American Writers*, edited by Harss and Barbara Dohmann, 102–36. New York: Harper & Row, 1966.
Ocampo, Victoria. *Diálogo con Borges.* Buenos Aires: Sur, 1969.
Sorrentino, Fernando. *Seven Conversations with Jorge Luis Borges*, translated by Clark M. Zlotchew. Troy N.Y.: Whitston Publishing Co., 1982.

Biography

Rodríguez Monegal, Emir. *Jorge Luis Borges: A Literary Biography.* New York: E. P. Dutton, 1978.

Critical Studies: Books

Aizenberg, Edna. *The Aleph Weaver: Biblical, Kabbalistic and Judaic Elements in Borges.* Potomac, Md.: Scripta Humanistica, 1984.
Alazraki, Jaime. *Borges and the Kabbalah and Other Essays on His Fiction and Poetry.* New York: Cambridge University Press, 1988.
———. *Jorge Luis Borges.* New York: Columbia University Press, 1971.
———. *La prosa narrativa de Jorge Luis Borges. Temas. Estilo.* Madrid: Gredos, 1968.
———. *Versiones. Inversiones. Reversiones. El espejo como modelo estructural del relato en los cuentos de Borges.* Madrid: Gredos, 1977.
Alazraki, Jaime, ed. *Critical Essays on Jorge Luis Borges.* Boston: G. K. Hall, 1987.
———. *Jorge Luis Borges.* Madrid: Taurus, 1976.
Barrenechea, Ana María. *La expresión de la irrealidad en la obra de Jorge Luis Borges.* Mexico City: Colegio de México, 1957. 2d ed., Buenos Aires: Paidós, 1967. Reprinted as *Borges the Labyrinth Maker.* New York: New York University Press, 1965.
Bastos, María Luisa. *Borges ante la crítica argentina 1923–1960.* Buenos Aires: Hispamérica, 1974.
Bell-Villada, Gene H. *Borges and His Fiction: A Guide to His Mind and Art.* Chapel Hill: University of North Carolina Press, 1981.
Bloom, Harold, ed. *Jorge Luis Borges.* New York: Chelsea House, 1986.

Christ, Ronald. *The Narrow Act: Borges' Art of Allusion.* New York: New York
University Press, 1969.
Cohen, J. M. *Jorge Luis Borges.* Edinburgh: Oliver & Boyd, 1973. New York:
Barnes & Noble, 1974.
Crossan, John Dominic. *Raid on the Articulate: Comic Eschatology in Jesus and
Borges.* New York: Harper & Row, 1976.
Dunham, Lowell, and Ivar Ivask, eds. *The Cardinal Points of Borges.* Norman:
University of Oklahoma Press, 1971.
Friedman, Mary Lusky. *The Emperor's Kites: A Morphology of Borges' Tales.*
Durham, N.C.: Duke University Press, 1987.
Goloboff, Gerardo Mario. *Leer Borges.* Buenos Aires: Huemul, 1978.
McMurray, George R. *Jorge Luis Borges.* New York: Ungar, 1980.
Molloy, Sylvia. *Las letras de Borges.* Buenos Aires: Sudamericana, 1979.
Rodríguez Monegal, Emir. *Borges, hacia una lectura poética.* Cover title *Borges,
hacia una interpretación.* Madrid: Guadarrama, 1976.
———. *Borges par lui-même.* Paris: Seuil, 1970. Reprinted as *Borges por él mismo.*
Caracas: Monte Avila, 1981.
———. *Jorge Luis Borges: A Literary Biography.* New York: E. P. Dutton, 1978.
Shaw, Donald L. *Borges: Ficciones.* London: Grant & Cutler, 1976.
Sosnowski, Saúl. *Borges y la Cábala: la búsqueda del verbo.* Buenos Aires: His-
pamérica, 1976. Buenos Aires: Pardés, 1986.
Stabb, Martin S. *Jorge Luis Borges.* New York: Twayne Publishers, 1970. New
York: St. Martin's Press, 1970.
Sturrock, John. *Paper Tigers: The Ideal Fictions of Jorge Luis Borges.* Oxford:
Clarendon Press, 1977.
Wheelock, Carter. *The Mythmaker: A Study of Motif and Symbol in the Short Stories
of Jorge Luis Borges.* Austin: University of Texas Press, 1969.

Critical Studies: Articles
Alazraki, Jaime. "Borges, or Style as an Invisible Worker." *Style* 9 (1975): 320–
34. Also in his *Borges and the Kabbalah*, 77–89.
———. "Génesis de un estilo: *Historia universal de la infamia.*" *Revista Iberoamericana* 123–24 (April-September 1983): 247–61. Also in his *Borges
and the Kabbalah* as "The Making of a Style: *A Universal History of Infamy,*"
90–104.
Barrenechea, Ana María. "Borges y la narración que se autoanaliza." In *Textos
hispanoamericanos: de Sarmiento a Sarduy*, 127–44. Caracas: Monte Avila,
1978.
———. "Borges y los símbolos." In *Textos hispanoamericanos*, 145–58.
Barth, John. "The Literature of Exhaustion." *Atlantic*, August 1967, 29–34.
Christ, Ronald. "A Modest Proposal for the Criticism of Borges." *Books Abroad*
45 (1971): 388–98.
Dauster, Frank. "Notes on Borges' Labyrinths." *Hispanic Review* 30 (April
1962): 142–48.

Selected Bibliography

Foster, David William. "Borges and Structuralism: Toward an Implied Poetics." *Modern Fiction Studies* 19, no. 3 (1973): 341–51.
———. "Toward a Characterization of *Écriture* in the Short Stories of Jorge Luis Borges." In his *Studies in the Contemporary Spanish-American Short Story*, 13–30. Columbia: University of Missouri Press, 1979.
Isaacs, Neil D. "The Labyrinth of Art in Four *Ficciones* of Jorge Luis Borges." *Studies in Short Fiction* 6 (1969): 383–94.
Johnson, William A. "The Sparagmos of Myth Is the Naked Lunch of Mode: Modern Literature as the Age of Frye and Borges." *Boundary* 8, no. 2 (1980): 297–311.
Lida de Malkiel, María Rosa. "Contribución al estudio de las fuentes literarias de Jorge Luis Borges." *Sur* 213–14 (July–August 1952): 50–57.
Man, Paul de. "A Modern Master." *New York Review of Books*, November 5, 1964: 8+. Reprinted in Bloom, ed., *Jorge Luis Borges*, 21–27.
Menton, Seymour. "Jorge Luis Borges, Magical Realist." *Hispanic Review* 50 (1982): 411–26.
Murillo, L. A. "The Labyrinths of Jorge Luis Borges, an Introductory [*sic*] to the Stories of *The Aleph*." *Modern Language Quarterly* 20 (1959): 259–66.
Phillips, Allen C. "Notas sobre Borges y la crítica reciente." *Revista Iberoamericana* 43 (January–June 1957): 41–59.
———. " 'El Sur' de Borges." *Revista Hispánica Moderna* 29 (1963): 140–47.
Scholes, Robert. "The Reality of Borges." In his *Fabulation and Metafiction*, 9–20. Urbana: University of Illinois Press, 1979.
Updike, John. "The Author as Librarian." *New Yorker*, 31 October 1965, 223–46.
Weber, Frances Weyers. "Borges's Stories: Fiction and Philosophy." *Hispanic Review* 36 (1968): 124–71.
Wheelock, Carter. "Borges and the 'Death' of the Text." *Hispanic Review* 53 (1985): 151–61.
———. "Borges, Courage and Will." *International Fiction Review* 2 (1975): 101–5.
———. "Borges's New Prose." *TriQuarterly* 25 (1972): 403–40.
———. "The Committed Side of Borges." *Modern Fiction Studies* 19 (1973): 373–79.
Zlotchew, Clark M. "The Collaboration of the Reader in Borges and Robbe-Grillet." *Michigan Academician* 14, no. 2 (1981): 167–73.
———. "Tlön, Llhuros, N. Daly, J. L. Borges." *Modern Fiction Studies* 19, no. 3 (1973): 453–59.

Special Periodical Issues
"40 inquisiciones sobre Borges." *Revista Iberoamericana* 100–1 (July–December 1977).
"Jorge Luis Borges." *Cahiers de L'Herne* [Paris] 4 (1964).
"Tribute Issue for Jorge Luis Borges." *Modern Fiction Studies* 19, no. 3 (1973).

TriQuarterly 25 (1972). Reprinted as *Prose for Borges*. Evanston, Ill.: Northwestern University Press, 1974.

Bibliographies

Balderston, Daniel. *The Literary Universe of Jorge Luis Borges: An Index to References and Allusions to Persons, Titles, and Places in His Writings*. New York: Greenwood Press, 1986.

Becco, Horacio Jorge. *Jorge Luis Borges: bibliografía total, 1923–1973*. Buenos Aires: Casa Pardo, 1973.

Foster, David William. *Jorge Luis Borges: An Annotated Primary and Secondary Bibliography*. Introduction by Martin S. Stabb. New York: Garland Press, 1984.

Index

Index

174

The Author

Naomi Lindstrom is professor of Spanish and Portuguese at the University of Texas at Austin, where she also works with the Institute of Latin American Studies. She is the author of *Literary Expressionism in Argentina* (1977), *Macedonio Fernández* (1981), *Jewish Issues in Argentine Literature: From Gerchunoff to Szichman* (1989), and *Women's Voice in Latin American Literature* (1989). Her English translations of literary works include the 1929 novel *The Seven Madmen* (1984) by the Argentine Roberto Arlt as well as collections of poetry by contemporary Latin American authors.

The Editor

Gordon Weaver earned his Ph.D. in English and creative writing at the University of Denver, and is currently professor of English at Oklahoma State University. He is the author of several novels, including *Count a Lonely Cadence, Give Him a Stone, Circling Byzantium*, and *The Eight Corners of the World*. His short stories are collected in *The Entombed Man of Thule, Such Waltzing Was Not Easy, Getting Serious, Morality Play*, and *A World Quite Round*. Recognition of his fiction includes the St. Lawrence Award for Fiction, two National Endowment for the Arts Fellowships, and the O. Henry First Prize. He edited *The American Short Story, 1945–1980; A Critical History* and is currently editor of the *Cimarron Review*. Married and the father of three daughters, he lives in Stillwater, Oklahoma.